BookMarks

Volume 5

Bible Explorations for Older Youth

Edited by
Sandra DeMott Hasenauer

Judson Press ▪ Valley Forge

BookMarks, Volume 5: Bible Explorations for Older Youth

Library of Congress Cataloging-in-Publication Data
    (Revised for volume 5)
Bible explorations for older youth / edited by Sandra DeMott Hasenauer.
    p.   cm.
Volume 5: ISBN 0-8710-1418-7 (pbk. : alk. paper)
Volume 4: ISBN 0-8170-1334-2 (pbk. : alk. paper)
Volume 3: ISBN 0-8170-1333-4 (pbk. : alk. paper)
Volume 2: ISBN 0-8170-1332-6 (pbk. : alk. paper)
Volume 1: ISBN 0-8170-1331-8 (pbk. : alk. paper)
1. Bible–Study and teaching.   2. Christian education of young people.   I. Hasenauer, Sandra DeMott.   II. Series: Bookmarks (Judson Press) ; v. 5.
BS600.2.B443 1999
220'.071'2—dc21   99-36852

Printed in the U.S.A.

08 07 06 05 04 03 02

10 9 8 7 6 5 4 3 2 1

Contents

~~~~~~

Welcome to *BookMarks,* a fresh idea in Bible study curriculum for older youth. *BookMarks* combines a high regard for the biblical story with respect for the honesty and thoughtfulness of older youth. The sessions in this volume are specifically designed to give youth access to the Bible in a way that challenges youth to discover meaning in the Bible for their own lives. You'll notice the difference right away!

BookMarks is designed for older youth as a part of the larger curriculum series, *Bible Quest: A Bible Story Curriculum for All Ages.* As part of the *Bible Quest* series, each volume of *BookMarks* will follow at least two of the four broad themes that emerge from the biblical story. These are: Covenant, Liberation and Justice, Salvation, and Incarnation.

The Story Is the Point

One of the greatest challenges for the church today is how to address the biblical illiteracy of young people who have grown up in the church. Many youth who have spent years in Sunday school and youth programs remember little about what is in the Bible. Although the Bible has been used to teach many lessons, youth seem to have missed the story behind the message—end of lesson, end of story! For *BookMarks,* the biblical story *is* the point! The objective of each session is to create an opportunity for youth to engage the story directly, so that the biblical story itself is what is remembered. Through this direct encounter with the Bible, the Bible story is joined to the story of our own lives, challenging our behavior, informing our decisions, and nurturing our relationship with God.

The Learner Is an Interpreter

BookMarks values the perspectives youth bring to their study of the Bible. Each session encourages youth to see the biblical story in light of their own lives. In addition, each session provides an opportunity for youth to practice using tools and approaches that contribute to responsible interpretation. As youth become familiar with the process of biblical interpretation, they are encouraged to consider the Bible an accessible resource for faith and life. As youth are able to see the connections between their own story and the biblical story, they discover meaning in that story and learn to look to Scripture as a resource for living now and in the future.

A Six-Step Process

The sessions in *BookMarks* use a six-step process to help youth engage the Bible story and find meaning in that story for their lives. Each step includes two options, so the leader can design the session especially for the needs of the youth. In "Setting the Stage," youth are welcomed into the interpretive process through activities and discussions that foreshadow key features of the story to be considered. In "Telling the Story," the story itself is presented in ways that will help youth to pay close attention to its plot, characters, and content. In "Reacting to the Story," youth are invited and helped to share their initial responses to the story, including their questions and their first impressions of its meaning. In "Connecting to the Story," youth are challenged to discover the intersection of the biblical story with their own lives, seeing themselves through the characters and situations of the Bible story and beginning to identify the personal relevance of the story. In "Exploring the Story," youth are introduced to various tools and approaches for responsible biblical interpretation, encouraging them to place their own understanding of the story in the context of the wider faith community. In "Living the Story," youth express their emerging sense of the meaning of the story for their lives in a closing context of affirmation and worship. In addition, each *BookMarks* session includes two reproducible handouts designed to contribute to the learning process.

Additional Features

In addition to the six-step process with two options in each step, *BookMarks* sessions include a number of other features to support the leader in the process of helping youth discover the relevance of Scripture for their lives. "A Story behind the Story" provides the leader with contextual information about the biblical story, describing important historical, cultural, and theological background to the story. "Possible Youth Contact Points" suggests some of the issues and questions important to youth that may become avenues of connection to the biblical story. "You May Need" provides an up-front look at the materials you may need to gather depending on the session options you choose. "Enter the Story" suggests a process for the leader's intentional engagement with the Bible story prior to leading the session, encouraging reflection that may contribute to the interpretive process. "Things to Ponder" helps the leader to be aware of possible issues for youth that may emerge or need further attention as a result of studying a particular Bible story. "Looking Ahead" helps the leader to anticipate those options in the next session that may need some extra preparation time.

The Writers for This Volume

CAROL S. ADAMS, a newlywed, takes time away from her spouse to write. Together they enjoy working with youth, camping, and eating cookies.

SANDRA DEMOTT HASENAUER is an American Baptist minister living in Rochester, New York, and currently serving as associate executive director for Resources and AB GIRLS for American Baptist Women in Valley Forge, Pennsylvania. In addition to editing and writing for this volume, Sandra edited Volumes 2, 4, and 6 of the *BookMarks* series.

PAUL MAST HEWITT has more than seven years of experience as minister to youth and children. Currently he serves as a family worker with Lifelink Head Start in West Chicago, Illinois.

DENISE JANSSEN is a bi-vocational American Baptist pastor serving as minister of Christian education and youth at Community Church of Wilmette, Illinois, and as director of development at Garrett-Evangelical Theological Seminary in Evanston, Illinois.

RENÉ RODGERS JENSEN is copastor of First Christian Church in Omaha, Nebraska, and a frequent contributor to curriculum projects related to the Christian Church, Disciples of Christ. She is wife of Rick and mother of Erica and Peter.

MARK LUERA is a frequent contributor to curriculum projects related to the Christian Church, Disciples of Christ. He lives in Corsicana, Texas, where he serves as senior minister of First Christian Church. Mark has also provided leadership in various youth ministry programs related to his denomination.

LAUREN NG KUSHNER formerly served on the staff of International Ministries, American Baptist Churches USA. A writer and editor, she has had experience with local church youth ministry, conference leadership and administration, and other positions of denominational leadership.

MARK RAMBO is associate pastor of First Baptist Church of Olympia, Washington. In addition to his ministry in the local church, he contributes leadership to numerous regional and national Christian education and youth ministry programs related to American Baptist Churches USA.

WALLACE R. SMITH is minister of outreach for the First Baptist Church of Indianapolis. An active leader and contributor to regional and national youth ministry in the American Baptist Churches USA, he lives with his wife, Christy, in Fishers, Indiana, where they recently celebrated the birth of their first child.

It is my sincere hope that you and your youth will enjoy these sixteen sessions as a fresh opportunity to consider the biblical story as full of meaning for our lives.

Grace and peace to you in Christ,

Sandra DeMott Hasenauer

Sandra DeMott Hasenauer
American Baptist Women
American Baptist Churches USA

1. Sarah Laughs

Bible Story: Genesis 18:1-15

Carol Adams

A Story behind the Story

Most of Genesis has to do with the carrying out of God's promise to Abraham. This covenant with Abraham is a central promise to several major world faiths: Christianity, Judaism, and Islam. The covenant (or promise) is first told in Genesis 12:2: "I will make of you a great nation," said God. This presupposes Abraham fathering children, however, and that soon became the issue. Years passed, and although Abraham remained childless, God continued to reiterate his promise (Genesis 15:1).

Sarah's own concern as to how the covenant would be secured led her to take matters into her own hands. Although she is often accused of disbelief by contemporary readers, it might be just as appropriate to interpret her decision as assuming that God's covenant would take place through human actions—simply another way to attempt to carry out God's will. It was not uncommon in the ancient Middle East for a barren wife to offer her concubine to her husband as a way to carry on the family name. Sarah's actions would not have been particularly shocking in her community. Although Ishmael was born (for further word of the problems that result, read Genesis 16), God continued to promise another child—and a child by Sarah, no less. The promise continued, even in the face of a distinct lack of evidence.

The story in Genesis 18 is still about covenant, about promise, about hope against all odds. Over that bedrock, however, are layers about justice and hospitality. The visitors come out of nowhere. Are they angels? We're not told. Abraham initially saw them as nothing but strangers coming across the desert, needing a safe place to break their journey. He provided food, companionship during their meal, and protection from harm while they were in his care.

What does this story have to say about God's justice? How do promise and liberation intermingle here? Did Sarah's laughter of disbelief stem from the same emotion we feel whenever we pick up a newspaper? "Sure, God's will might eventually be done on earth, but I'm seeing no sign of it right now!" How are visiting strangers the emissaries of God to us? All of these questions, and more, can be raised by today's passage.

Enter the Story

If you have time, you might want to read the entire story of Abraham and the covenant cycle, which extends from Genesis 11:27 to 25:11. Where do you see covenant and justice intermingled? If you can only read today's passage, make sure you give it time to sink in. Put yourself in Sarah's shoes and read the story from her point of view. Consider this: have you ever wanted to laugh in disbelief at something you felt God was saying to you?

1

POSSIBLE YOUTH CONTACT POINTS

- Do I ever lie out of fear?
- When things are difficult, how can I trust God's promise that nothing is too difficult for God?
- Is it possible to see God's face in a stranger?
- Where do I see God's promise being carried out in the world?

YOU MAY NEED

- newsprint
- markers
- advertisements from magazines
- prerecorded videotape of an infomercial or collection of TV commercials (optional)
- TV and VCR (optional)
- a tent
- Bibles—several translations
- "IQ Test" handouts
- writing utensils
- blank or writing paper
- several copies of current newspapers and news magazines
- poster board (number of sheets depending on size of group)
- glue
- scissors
- "Nothing Is Too Difficult" handouts
- 3″ x 5″ index cards
- candle
- matches or lighter

Setting the Stage (5–10 minutes)

OPTION A

Needed: newsprint, markers

Gather students and welcome them. Tell them that at the end of the session, anyone who answers every question correctly will receive $1 million. Clarify that the money is not for the person who answers the *most* questions correctly but only for those who answer *every* question correctly. Ask:

- Does this seem like a reasonable promise? Why or why not?
- Which end of the bargain do you think will be the hardest to hold up—you answering every question correctly or me giving you the money?

Explain that some of the questions in the session may not have any right or wrong answers. Either way, you do not have a million dollars to hand out. After establishing that your promise is impossible to fulfill, continue the discussion. Get several responses to the following questions:

- Has anyone ever promised you something that you thought was impossible?
- How did you react?

Ask several students to give a definition for the word *promise*. Record their responses on the newsprint. Challenge the group to adopt a thorough definition for use throughout the study. Once a definition is established, continue on with these questions:

- Are promises conditional?
- What makes a promise believable or not believable?

Say: *The people in today's Bible story heard a pretty unbelievable promise. Let's see how they reacted.*

OPTION B

Needed: magazine advertisements or video of infomercial or commercials, TV and VCR (optional)

Bring in several ads that promise results if you use their product. If you can find a video of a good infomercial or collection of TV commercials, play it as students arrive. Show the students the ads. Highlight sections that promise unbelievable results.

Ask learners to tell about similar offers they have seen or heard. Encourage them to share offers that seem too good to be true. When several youth have shared, use these questions to spark a discussion:

- What do these promises have in common?
- How do you react to such claims?

Say: *The people in today's Bible story heard a pretty unbelievable promise. Let's see how they reacted.*

Telling the Story (5–10 minutes)

OPTION A

Needed: tent, Bibles

Before students arrive, set up your tent in your meeting place. For variety, you may want to set up in a different room or outside.

Gather the youth near the tent. Inform them that they just arrived on the scene of an interesting story found in Scripture. Not only are they at the scene, but they are actually going to relive the story. Open your Bible to Genesis 18:1-15. As you read aloud, assign participants to act out the story as you read it. You may wish to read a line and then pause for the characters to act it out. Encourage them to say the lines as if they were really the characters in the story. When finished, show appreciation to the "cast" with a round of applause.

Invite everyone to open their Bibles to Genesis 18. Ask a volunteer to read Genesis 18:1-15 one more time out loud.

OPTION B
Needed: several translations of the Bible
Pass out different versions of the Bible to the students. Depending on the size of your group, you may wish to divide into pairs or triads. Take some time to explain how the translations differ. Point out that some versions were translated with attention to each original word in the manuscript. Others try to get the main idea across, with less emphasis placed on each individual word.

Have each person or group open their translation to Genesis 18:1-15. Have them silently read through the passage in their version. After all have finished, invite a few to read their version out loud. Discuss similarities and differences among the various readings. You don't need to read out loud every version. Yet be sure that any versions that are especially unusual get shared with the entire group. Discuss which versions were more difficult to comprehend and which ones were easier.

Reacting to the Story (10–15 minutes)
OPTION A
Needed: "IQ Test" handouts, writing utensils, Bibles, newsprint and markers (optional)
Give each participant a copy of the "IQ Test" handout. Explain that

this is an easy way to begin studying the Bible. This format is helpful in responding to the passages they read.

Read each section of the handout. Tell the students that they can use this technique for any passage they read. The handout suggests reading the passage three times. Your group just finished reading or hearing it at least twice. Suggest that they silently review it at least one more time on their own.

Give them time to write down a few things for each section. Ask volunteers to share insights. Be sure to affirm their responses. Then ask volunteers to share their questions. Suggest that perhaps some of these questions will get answered before the end of the session. You might record the questions on newsprint to refer to later.

OPTION B
Needed: paper, writing utensils
Invite learners to imagine that the story they just heard happened recently in their community.

Divide them into groups. (Smaller classes may choose to stay as one group.) Inform them that each group represents a news station in your area. Their job is to get the top news story for the evening news. Give them time to prepare a short skit in which the news reporters interview Abraham and Sarah. Encourage them to use props from whatever they may find in the classroom to make it more realistic.

Challenge them to think as a reporter would—to get the real juicy scoop! You may wish to prompt them on some angles to explore. Here are some examples:

- Do Abraham and Sarah tell the same version of the incident?
- How did Abraham react?
- Why did Sarah lie about her reaction?
- Who were these men, and what did Abraham and Sarah feel about them when they first saw them?
- Had they had other experiences with unexpected visitors needing to be fed?
- Where did the men go after they left Abraham and Sarah's tent? Did they just eat and run?

After several minutes, gather the news teams together to share their news reports with the whole group.

Connecting to the Story (10–15 minutes)

OPTION A

Share a story about a time when someone told you something that you found to be unbelievable. Perhaps you even thought the other person was joking. After you heard the news, you laughed. Later, though, you found out the news was true. Choose a story the learners can relate to. Practice telling it with animation so the learners are drawn into the story immediately.

After sharing, invite the learners to share their own stories as well, reminding them that this is exactly what happened to Sarah. Get responses from several of the youth, if not from the entire group. Encourage everyone to listen to each other to avoid side conversations and stories.

Ask the learners if any of them was ever promised something so unbelievable that they laughed when they heard it. Give your own example, if possible, to set the tone. Invite sharing among the group. Encourage them to share promises that they actually did receive, even though they seemed unreasonable.

Remind students that laughing is a common response when things seem unbelievable.

OPTION B

Needed: current newspapers and news magazines, poster board, glue, scissors, markers

Offer to the group some of the information from "A Story behind the Story," about God's promises and the reality of our world. The Bible promises us that God's will ultimately will be done, that God's justice will prevail.

Abraham and Sarah were asked to believe a promise in the face of a distinct lack of evidence. The reality belied the promise at the time, yet God's promise did come true.

Offer the group the newspapers and other supplies. If you have a larger group, consider breaking into triads or foursomes for this activity. Invite the group(s) to first find stories that illustrate injustices, oppression, or wrongdoing and put them on the poster board. Then, after giving them a few minutes to do so, ask them to go through the same newspapers to find examples of ways that God's promise of justice and liberation is being carried out in the world today, and put them onto the same poster. They may be creative with how they do this, decorating the poster in any way they choose to show how God's promise can be believed today.

Exploring the Story
(10–15 minutes)
OPTION A

Needed: newsprint, markers, Bibles
Sarah wasn't the only one who laughed when she heard God's promise. Invite the group to turn to Genesis 17. Have a volunteer read Genesis 17:15-21. Discuss the following questions as a group:

■ What are the similarities between the two passages?
■ What are the differences?
■ How did God respond to Abraham after he laughed?
■ How did God respond to Sarah after she laughed?
■ How do you think Abraham responded to Sarah after she laughed?

You may wish to write some of the responses on newsprint.

OPTION B

Needed: "Nothing Is Too Difficult" handouts, writing utensils, Bibles
Using your own words, say to the youth something like the following: *When Sarah heard the Lord say she would have a son, she reacted with laughter. The Lord then responded by saying, "Is anything too difficult for the Lord?"* Then ask: *It is easy to say, "Nothing is too difficult for the Lord," yet can we truly believe that is true? How does the Bible shed light on this idea?*

Pass out the "Nothing Is Too Difficult" handouts and writing utensils. Make sure each learner has a Bible handy. For the "Verses" section, assign students to read a verse out loud to the group. Have everyone write down the main idea of the verse on the handout. Encourage the learners to share their responses to the verses. Don't hesitate to look at the greater context surrounding the verses if students desire to do so.

For the "Stories" section, divide your group into four smaller groups (a "group" may be one person) or have students work as partners. Assign each passage in the "Stories" section to a group. Instruct them to read the passage and write on the handout how this passage demonstrates the idea that nothing is too difficult for the Lord.

Allow time for students to study their passage. After all groups are finished, invite a member from each group to share his or her findings with everyone. Encourage all learners to jot down the main ideas on their handouts.

Ask the youth to reflect upon this exercise. Pose questions such as these:

■ Based on this exercise, how would you describe God?
■ What areas in your life seem too difficult even for God to handle?
■ What about world issues—are any of those too complicated even for God?
■ How can these verses help you?

Living the Story
(5–10 minutes)
OPTION A

Needed: CD of instrumental music, CD player
Invite the learners to stand in a circle. Play some mellow instrumental music in the background. Ask the youth to think of a situation in their life that might be particularly difficult for them right now. Or, they can think about issues of justice that seem particularly challenging

to them personally. Invite the youth to silently consider the particulars of this personal issue or involvement in these justice issues.

After a moment, remind the group that nothing is too difficult for God. Have everyone turn around so that each person's back is toward the center of the circle. At this point no one will be able to look directly at anyone else. Tell them that this time is for them to spend individually with God. Encourage them to give over their difficult areas to God, or questions about their involvement in a larger issue, and ask for God's help. They may wish to kneel, put their hands out, or perform some other action to symbolize the giving of their difficulties to God or seeking God's guidance in commitment. After a while, you may wish to focus them all together by singing an appropriate song or closing with a group prayer.

OPTION B
Needed: 3" x 5" cards, pens, candle, matches or lighter
Gather the group together and instruct them to sit on the floor in a circle. Place the candle in the center and light it. Invite the group to reflect upon the lesson. Review the key discussion points of the lesson: God's promises in the face of reality, our own issues of belief or disbelief, etc.

Tell the group that now has come the time of commitment for each one of them. Pass out 3" x 5" cards and pens. Ask them to write down one or two things that they will commit to as a result of study-ing this lesson (some possible commitments might be "I will ask for God's help to believe the unbelievable promises" and "I will be a part of God's liberation in the world by . . .").

Encourage them to take general commitments (such as the ones listed) and come up with at least one specific way to live it out.

After all have written their commitments, close in a prayer. Invite learners to pray silently or out loud, asking for God's help in carrying out their commitments.

Things to Ponder
Which sections did the learners connect with most? Which sections did not work as well? Depending on family situations, some youth may have difficulty with the concept of "believable promises." Perhaps they've felt let down too many times. These are the youth who might need to hold on to God's promises the most. Give them a call or write them a note of encouragement. Pray for each student by name before the next session.

Looking Ahead
Depending on which options you choose, there are several opportunities in the next session to invite special guests to the classroom to participate in different steps. Be sure to invite these people far enough in advance to allow them time to prepare. The session also provides an opportunity for you to act as an illusionist. If you choose to do so, you will need to find yourself an illusion and practice it until you are able to perform it convincingly.

IQ Test

An easy way to begin studying a Scripture passage is to give it the IQ Test.

Begin by reading the passage three times. (It helps to read it out loud at least one of those times.)

Insights

Record any insights you have about the passage. An insight may be simple observations about the passage: who is writing, where the story takes place, etc. It may also be anything that particularly stands out to you.

Questions

Write down any questions you have about the passage. The questions may be about the story line, new words, or even how the passage applies to your life today.

Nothing Is Too Difficult

Verses:

1 Kings 8:56

Mark 14:36

Luke 1:37

Romans 4:21

Ephesians 3:20

Stories:

Genesis 6:13; 7:17-24

Daniel 3:11-28

John 11:14-17,38-44

Mark 4:35-41

2. The Widow's Oil

Bible Story: 2 Kings 4:1-37

Carol Adams

A Story behind the Story

Today's story, as in the story from the previous session, shows the power of God's promises—in particular, God's concern for the poor.

The story of Elisha's anointing as prophet may be found in 1 Kings 19, and Elisha's succession of Elijah as the preeminent prophet of God is recorded in 2 Kings 2. After Elijah was taken up into heaven, Elisha immediately began his ministry. He was well known, even at first, because of his connection with Elijah. Even the other prophets bowed to him, acknowledging him as their leader after Elijah's departure.

Both Elijah and Elisha were well-respected prophets, though their ministries were distinctly different. Elijah fought a king and priests and lived apart from the people. In contrast, Elisha lived among the people. He preferred working with the poor and widows, showing them God's love and concern for the oppressed.

Today's Scripture story is actually two stories combined. Bible scholars are careful to not only look at each story individually but to see how the two stories may expand upon each other. We have two women needing help: the first a poor widow, the second a wealthy wife. Despite their differences in socio-economic situation, however, both women were faithful believers in the power of God. They each knew immediately to go to Elisha for help when tragedy befell them. The widow needed to save her children from slavery in repayment of debts. The wealthy woman needed to save her son from death. In both stories, the children need to be liberated by God's power. In both stories, the women's faith led them to beseech the prophet's mediating power of God.

When we believe in God's power, great things can happen. Abundance appears where there was lack; life appears in the face of death. Do we literally believe in the biblical accounts of miracles? That's a personal decision. But can we take meaning from miracle stories regardless? Certainly. Where in our world can we find God's abundance? Where do we need to see life? How well do we believe God's promises of liberation?

Enter the Story

Consider lighting a candle and spending some time in prayer before you begin reading. After you've done so, picture yourself in the role of one of the characters, such as the widow, Gehazi, or even Elisha, and consider the story through those eyes. Finally, pray again that God might enlighten your mind with wisdom.

Setting the Stage
(5–10 minutes)

OPTION A

(If you choose this option, you will want to choose Option A of "Connecting to the Story.")
Needed: snacks, "hosts," visitor with gifts
Arrange ahead of time to have one or more student leaders arrive early.

POSSIBLE YOUTH CONTACT POINTS

- How can I be hospitable to those around me?
- How is God at work around me?
- How can I experience God's miracles in my life?
- Where does God's liberating power need to be seen in the world?

YOU MAY NEED

- snacks
- students to act as "hosts"
- visitor with gifts
- illusion or illusionist
- Bibles
- storyteller
- "IQ Test" handouts
- writing utensils
- newsprint and markers (optional)
- "It Didn't Work Out" handouts
- Bible study helps, such as Bible dictionaries, concordances, and commentaries
- stick-on name tags
- pens
- 3″ x 5″ cards
- candle
- matches or lighter

Their job is to welcome all the other students as they arrive. They will be the "hosts." Provide snacks and drinks for the hosts to offer the group. Encourage the hosts to selflessly meet any need that arises—really going out of their way to make everyone comfortable. If possible, arrange to have a key church leader, perhaps the pastor, arrive as well. Instruct the visitor to graciously accept the hospitality. Allow the group to fellowship and enjoy the hospitality of the hosts.

Signal the visitor as you are about to begin the lesson. This person will excuse himself or herself to allow the study to begin. Have the visitor, on the way out, give each host a gift to thank them for their hospitality. (The gift could be something small and symbolic, or it could simply be a note of thanks.) Thank the hosts for their servanthood.

OPTION B
Needed: illusion trick or an illusionist
Prior to the session, hook up with an illusionist or head to your local magic store. Practice at least one illusion so that you can perform it well. (No need to don the cape or pull any bunnies out of your hat!)

One great illusion involves an illusionist pouring water out of a pitcher until no more water is left. Suddenly, the illusionist is thirsty and grabs a cup. Miraculously, he or she pours more water out of the pitcher until it is empty. This is repeated again. The pitcher seems to refill on its own.

The trick is that the pitcher has different compartments. Each time it is poured, the illusionist grabs it from a different side. Only the

water from that side pours out, and the pitcher appears empty. One would think it is a miracle!

This water pitcher illusion would fit in splendidly with the story of the woman and the jars of oil. Yet many illusions can tie into the discussion on miracles. See what you can find and what you can perfect before the session. Have fun with it! This could be your chance to shine (or fall flat on your face, whichever!).

Telling the Story (5–10 minutes)
OPTION A
Needed: Bibles
Divide the students into three groups. Assign each group one of the following passages in 2 Kings 4: verses 1-7; verses 8-17; verses 18-37. Have each group act out their passage for the rest of the group. Give each group time to read the passage and prepare their skits. You may wish to encourage them to add a modern twist to the story. For example, the woman with the oil could be a woman with petroleum, Chanel No. 5, or even Pepsi—any liquid that would be of value in today's marketplace. Encourage them to sustain the main ideas of the story while having fun and exhibiting creativity. Brainstorm some creative ideas ahead of time in case some of the groups have difficulty getting started. Also, be prepared for the groups that will have so much fun that you will wonder if they read the same passage you did.

After each group presents its skit, review the real story. Instruct the learners to open their Bibles to 2 Kings 4. Summarize each section, or have someone read it aloud to the group. You may wish to read it one section at a time, followed by a brief summary of each section.

OPTION B
Needed: storyteller, Bibles
Invite a gifted storyteller to share the story of 2 Kings 4:1-37. Encourage the storyteller to paint a vivid picture of the scenes. The goal is to draw the listeners in so they become a part of the story, as if they were watching it happen right in front of them. Encourage the storyteller to be as creative as possible. Perhaps he or she will want to make it interactive, using students to act out different parts.

If a storyteller is not available, choose a learner who is an expressive reader. (Drama students are great!) Have this learner read the story aloud to the group. You may even encourage the listeners to close their eyes as they hear the story. Encourage them to picture the story in their mind as it is read. As the passage is quite long, you may wish to skip over a few details. Another option would be to write a summary of the story and have your reader read that instead.

After the story is told, have listeners open their Bibles to 2 Kings 4. Summarize each section of the story, or have them read it if it was summarized earlier.

Reacting to the Story (10–15 minutes)
OPTION A
Needed: "IQ Test" handouts, writing utensils, Bibles, newsprint and markers (optional)
Give each participant a copy of the "IQ Test" handout. If you used this handout from the previous lesson,

simply review the procedure and let them begin. If this is the first time using this handout, explain that this is an easy way to begin studying the Bible. This format is helpful in responding to the passages they read.

Read each section of the handout. Tell the students that they can use this technique for any passage they read. The handout suggests reading the passage three times. Your group just finished reading or hearing it at least twice. Suggest that they silently review it at least one more time on their own.

Give them time to write down a few things for each section. Ask volunteers to share insights. It will be fun to see the variety of responses! Be sure to affirm their differing responses. Then ask volunteers to share their questions. Encourage them by suggesting that perhaps some of these questions will get answered before the end of the session. You may even wish to record the questions on newsprint to refer to later.

OPTION B
Needed: Bibles
Have the group work individually or in pairs. Assign each person or group to be one of the characters in the story. If you have enough people, it would be great to have more than one person or group for each character. If you have fewer people, focus on the major characters. Assign the following characters: the widow, the widow's children, Elisha, the Shunammite woman, the Shunammite woman's husband, and Gehazi.

Instruct each person or group to put themselves in the place of the character. Have them discuss what their character would be thinking and feeling in each section of the story. Encourage them to think about how they would have reacted if they were that character. What would they have done differently? What other choices might each character have made? How would those choices change the outcome of the story?

When all groups have had sufficient time, bring the entire group together. Discuss one character at a time. Allow each person or group assigned to that character to share first. Then encourage feedback from the rest of the learners.

Connecting to the Story (10–15 minutes)
OPTION A
(Choose this option if you used Option A for "Setting the Stage.")
Refer to the beginning activity involving the "hosts" and the visitor. Discuss the following as a group: *What are the similarities and differences between what happened with our "hosts" and what happened with the Shunammite woman when she acted as a host?* Some questions to help the comparison are these:
■ Whose idea was it to host?
■ What did they sacrifice in order to host?
■ Did those hosting expect anything in return?
■ What did they get in return?
■ For how long did they host?

After you've spent some time on the comparison, ask the youth to consider times when they were asked to host someone. Ask:
■ What was it like?
■ Did you have to sacrifice any-

thing (for example, your bedroom for your grandmother's visit)?
■ Was it hard to do so? Why or why not?
■ What did you receive in return?
■ What if the guest were a complete stranger—would that have changed anything?

Compare today's story with the story of Abraham and Sarah hosting the visitors in the Genesis passage from the last session and with their own stories of hosting. Ask: *What are the similarities and differences?*

OPTION B
Needed: "It Didn't Work Out" handouts
Give each learner a copy of the handout "It Didn't Work Out." Have a volunteer read the scenario out loud while the rest of the group follows along. Brainstorm a list of all the possible ways that Jackie might have responded to this situation.

In pairs or triads, have students share about times when they got something they wanted but it did not work out the way they imagined. Have them share how they responded to the situations. Give learners enough time for each person to share. Then point the group back to the story of the Shunammite woman. Ask:
■ What did she receive that was promised to her?
■ How did it not work out as she thought it might?
■ How did she respond?
■ Do you think this was her first response or just what was recorded? Why?

Now have each learner think back to his or her own story. Ask:
■ Based on how the Shunammite woman responded in the story,

how do you think she would have responded if she were in your situation?

- How would you respond if the same situation happened to you again?

Exploring the Story (10–15 minutes)

OPTION A

Needed: Bibles, Bible study helps

This passage mentions several miracles: the jars of oil, the promised son, and the awakening of the son. Whether or not someone believes in the literal occurrence of biblical miracles, we can still take away from these stories truths about God's will, God's love, and God's power for good in the world.

Divide the learners into smaller groups. Encourage each group to find out as much as they can about miracles. Provide the Bible study helps to the group. Encourage the group to use them to study what the Bible says about miracles as well as what other writers say.

Some possible discussion points might include the following:

- Compare and contrast the miracles in this passage to other miracles recorded in the Bible.
- How would you define a miracle?
- What truths do these biblical stories of miracles teach us about the nature of God?
- Do miracles happen today?

OPTION B

Needed: Bibles

Gather the learners with their Bibles. Challenge them to answer this question: *Where is God in this story?* Have them skim back through the passage and write down how many times God is mentioned in the story.

When all have had a chance to explore, gather responses. Lead the group in a discussion using the following statements and questions:

- Was God mentioned by name?
- How was God mentioned in other ways?
- The Shunammite woman called Elisha a "holy man of God." How did she know he was a holy man?
- Elisha also exhibited much power. He instructed the widow to pour out her oil, and it was overflowing. Later, he promised the Shunammite woman a son, and it was so. When the son died, Elisha revived him. Where did his power come from? Was it his power or God's power? Is there any way to know for sure?

Invite the youth to explore some other verses on God's power (perhaps assigning different passages to different pairs of youth): Exodus 9:13-17; Exodus 14:15-22; Luke 24:44-49; Acts 1:8-9; 2 Timothy 1:5-7.

Ask: *How do these verses have impact upon how we look at the 2 Kings passage?*

Living the Story (5–10 minutes)

OPTION A

(Choose this option if you used Option A for "Connecting to the Story.")

Needed: Stick-on name tags, pens

Refresh the group's memory on how the "hosts" selflessly served the group. Remind them also of how the Shunammite woman selflessly hosted Elisha, a holy man of God.

Tell the learners that they now have an opportunity to commit to being hosts to holy people. Remind them that God loves every person and desires for them to grow in holiness. Thus, when we practice hospitality to those around us, we are serving the ones God loves. Through our service, we may be helping others to grow in holiness.

Give each learner a stick-on name tag. Explain that hosts often wear name tags. This name tag is a symbol of how we are each called to be hospitable. Instruct participants to write on their tags some specific ways that they can be "hosts" to those around them. Perhaps they will be nicer to their siblings or say hello to the shy kids at school. Give them time to write at least two specific ways they can be hospitable.

Invite learners to share some of their ideas, then close in a prayer together.

OPTION B
Needed: 3" x 5" cards, pens, candle, matches or lighter
If you chose this option for the previous lesson, remind the learners of this ritual time of commitment. Gather the group together and instruct them to sit on the floor in a circle. Place the candle in the center and light it. Invite the group to reflect on the lesson. Review the key discussion points of the lesson: the woman and the oil, the response of the Shunammite woman, how God's love and power were exhibited throughout the story, etc.

Tell the group that now has come the time of commitment for each one of them. Pass out 3" x 5" cards and pens. Ask them to write down one or two things that they will commit to as a result of studying this lesson. Encourage them to take general commitments and come up with at least one specific way to live it out.

After all have written their commitments, close in a prayer. Invite learners to pray silently or out loud, asking for God's help in carrying out their commitments.

Things to Ponder
Assess how each section of the session went. Compare with the session from last time. Note the students' abilities to see God in the story. Do you think they will effectively transfer the concept into personally seeing God in their own lives? Also, note which students are naturally hospitable in your group. Send them a note of encouragement this week. Consider sending notes of encouragement to all the youth in living out any commitments they made in "Living the Story."

Looking Ahead
Depending on which options you choose, you may need to prepare word sheets for the song "Down by the Riverside" or acquire a recording of the song itself. You may also need to prepare a path to the classroom as described in "Setting the Stage," Option B. A later option requires an adult volunteer to be prepared to act the role of Micah while telling the Scripture story. This person will need plenty of time to prepare, so be sure to invite him as far in advance as possible.

IQ Test

An easy way to begin studying a Scripture passage is to give it the IQ Test.

Begin by reading the passage three times. (It helps to read it out loud at least one of those times.)

nsights

Record any insights you have about the passage. An insight may be simple observations about the passage: who is writing, where the story takes place, etc. It may also be anything that particularly stands out to you.

uestions

Write down any questions you have about the passage. The questions may be about the story line, new words, or even how the passage applies to your life today.

It Didn't Work Out

Jackie always loved playing softball. She remembers sweating many hours out in the backyard with her brothers. Jackie was playing on any team she could as soon as it was available. Sometimes she was even on more than one team at a time.

In high school she made the team easily. She was always a good player but never the star player. Yet she worked her hardest to improve. She spent extra hours swinging the bat and diligently got up every morning at 5:30 in order to partake in her daily five-mile run.

Finally, in her senior year, Jackie was elected to be the captain of her team. She was so excited! The first game of the season, she was selected to start the game as the first batter. The pitch came, she swung, and it was out of the field! Excitedly, she headed toward first. As she rounded the base, suddenly she felt a jerk and a sharp pain before falling to the ground.

Jackie's knee had popped out of joint. It was ugly. After a visit to the doctor, it was determined that Jackie would be in physical therapy for quite awhile. The chances were slim that she would be able to play another game that season.

How might Jackie respond to this situation?

3. The Coming Reign of God
Bible Story: Micah 4:1-8

Sandra DeMott Hasenauer

A Story behind the Story

Few of us manage to grow to adulthood without hearing these words from Micah spoken or sung with hope:

> They shall beat their swords into plowshares,
> and their spears into pruning hooks:
> nation shall not lift up sword against nation,
> neither shall they learn war any more. (Micah 4:3)

It is notable, especially, that these words are carved into the wall at the United Nations building in New York City. The UN certainly gets caught up in its own politics, and it gets as tied up in bureaucracy as any other governmental organization, but it was founded with the hope that nations would actively pursue peace in their dealings with each other and that humans would ultimately find ways to live with each other in unity.

This is a hope that has sustained humankind since history first began to be written.

The Book of Micah is truly an exercise in faith, as we are bombarded by jolting messages of blame and dire warnings of the bleak future in store for Jerusalem, alternating with glorious words of hope. The hinge pin upon which these words twist? Walking the paths of righteousness, the path of God. In this Scripture, it is clear that if we walk the ways God would have us walk, God's peace would reign.

Micah launched angry words at the leaders of Judea, holding them responsible for the suffering of the poor. The rich exploited the vulnerable; the gap between rich and poor was growing wider every day. The government spent more money on arms than on agricultural improvement, choosing to outfit their armies rather than feed their starving. In addition, to keep a powerful rival country in abeyance, Judea was paying tribute—vast sums of money—to Assyria. That money was raised from the backs of the laborers.

Suddenly, history doesn't seem quite so distant. So many nations in the world today (arguably including our own) walk this tightrope between grain and guns, too often veering to the side of armaments. Micah's reminder is that there is no net there, no safety in ignoring the plight of the poor. Ultimately, that lack of caring will bring the nation down. A hungry people is a weak people, ripe for being conquered and exiled.

The words of hope we hear in this passage, lifting our hearts and calling us to action, seem to ring even louder as we think of the risen Christ. The Son of God walked among us, preaching peace and challenging us to justice. How well we should hear these words now!

POSSIBLE YOUTH CONTACT POINTS

- Where are God's paths of righteousness in my life?
- Is world peace truly possible?
- What is my role in living God's vision of peace?

YOU MAY NEED

- Bibles
- musical recording or instruments and song sheets to play "Down by the Riverside" or some other protest song
- several 8½" x 11" sheets of paper, each with a single word and an arrow on it (as described in "Setting the Stage" Option B), laid in a path from some distant point to your classroom
- volunteer actor for the role of Micah
- blank paper
- writing utensils
- "Who Is Like God?" handouts
- poster board
- markers
- glue
- current newspapers and news and current events magazines (*Time, Christian Century, Newsweek*, etc.)
- "What's Going On?" handouts
- Bible study helps, such as concordances, commentaries, and Bible dictionaries, encyclopedias, and atlases
- hymnals or songbooks (optional)
- banner-making materials, such as fabric, scissors, glue, other decorative elements

Enter the Story

If you're a child of the sixties, you may well remember a few good protest songs. Consider singing one or two to yourself (yes, out loud, if you are alone or don't mind someone hearing you!) before sitting down to read Micah 4:1-8. Consider your own role in bringing about God's peace. What are the "weapons"—words, actions, attitudes—that you use each day to bring others down? Pray for God's love to reign in your heart, and consider God's call to peace contained in Scripture. (If using this session during the Advent season, you might also want to consider singing or playing a recording of "O Little Town of Bethlehem," reading Micah 5:2-5, then returning to Micah 4:1-8 again.)

Setting the Stage (5–10 minutes)

OPTION A

Needed: musical recording of (or instruments and song sheets to play) "Down by the Riverside" or some other protest song

Using a recording or an accompanist, or playing the songs yourself, open by singing together "Down by the Riverside" (the words of which are drawn directly from today's passage) or some other popular song that celebrates peace. It could be that the youth are unfamiliar with the song; if so, why not take a few minutes to teach them? Feel free to have fun with rhythm, making variations to bring it more in line with what your youth might enjoy. However, don't worry too much about its sounding dated. Youth generally

appreciate the chance to learn "retro" music.

After singing together, inform the class that today's session will be about following God's path of peace in our lives. Then have an opening prayer together.

OPTION B

Needed: paper with arrows and phrases laid in a path (described below)

Ahead of class, lay a path of paper "stepping-stones" that will lead the youth toward the classroom from whatever point you choose (perhaps the sanctuary or fellowship hall—wherever they will have been just prior to class). On the papers, write single words or short phrases that might be used to describe God's paths, such as *peace, love, wisdom, caring, righteousness, compassion,* etc. (If you choose to cover a long distance, consider repeating words you feel are particularly important. Or use the word *peace* several times, interspersed among the other words, to lift it up as today's central concept.) On each piece of paper, along with the word, draw a bold arrow that points in the direction of the next stepping-stone.

Don't call the youths' attention to the stones prior to the class; allow them to make the discovery themselves. When the youth arrive in the classroom, ask if they noticed the path. If so, what are their thoughts? Do they have any questions? Comments? After just a couple of moments discussing the path (during which you do not offer any explanation or answers), inform the class that you'll be looking at a passage that talks about God's paths of righteousness and peace. Have a prayer together.

Telling the Story
(5–10 minutes)
OPTION A
Needed: adult volunteer, Bibles
If you have a man in the congregation who is a particularly effective actor, invite him to the classroom to present Micah 4:1-8 to the class as if he were actually the prophet Micah giving it as an original prophecy. He should dress the part and memorize the Scripture to make it more effective. If he has the time, it would add to the realism if your actor studied some of the historical background to the prophecy and used that as a part of his drama. He could, for example, begin by verbally setting up the youth in the class as if they were the poor of his village. Then he could talk with them about the situation of the country and the abuses of the leaders prior to launching into his prophecy. After your guest is done prophesying and departs, have the youth read the passage again from the New Revised Standard Version.

OPTION B
Needed: blank paper, writing utensils
Give each youth a blank piece of paper and pencil and make sure they have a hard writing surface available to them. Invite them to get comfortable and, if you have room, separate themselves somewhat from each other so they are not distracted. Let them know that you're about to read the session's theme passage. Instruct them to either draw or jot down words or phrases about the passage as they

hear it. Their drawing might be an illustration of the images of the Scripture or an image of their own reaction to it. The words or phrases might be ones from the Scripture that particularly jump out to them as they listen, or they might be connections or questions they have during the reading. Let the youth know as well that you will be reading the passage twice, with some time of silence between. They are to remain silent and refrain from distracting their classmates during the entire reading process, but they may draw or write as much as they want during the entire time, as long as it remains focused on the Scripture.

Read the Scripture through twice, giving it as much natural inflection (and making it sound prophetic) as you can. Allow for a few moments of silence between the two readings.

Reacting to the Story
(10–15 minutes)
OPTION A
(This option would be particularly effective if you used Option A in "Telling the Story.")
Invite the youth to consider themselves the original hearers of this prophecy. Using some of the historical information given in "A Story behind the Story," or any you've discovered in your own research, help the youth to understand what it would have been like to live in a small town outside of Jerusalem at the time of Micah's activity. They would be poor, oppressed, routinely shaken down for higher taxes; their country would be in imminent danger of being conquered by a large, powerful neighboring country; etc. Feel free to read some of Micah's

other prophecies, those focusing on bleak warnings and doom (Micah 2 has some particularly good sections for this). Invite the youth to discuss aloud, then, how they might feel hearing the words of hope from Micah 4:1-8, given the situation of their lives.

OPTION B
(This option is the follow-up to Option B in "Telling the Story.") After you have finished reading the passage twice, still remaining in silence, invite the youth to do the following: if they've created a drawing, ask them to place themselves somewhere in the drawing that is meaningful to them. Are they a part of the action, as it were, or are they standing off to the side and observing? Are they worshipping, beating swords into plowshares, or walking in the path of God? Or are they using weapons against others? For the youth who have been using words, invite them to add a few words to their paper that might reflect how they feel the passage directly relates to them. What message is it sending?

Invite the youth to each get with a partner, or if your class is a manageable size, come back into the group as a whole and share as much of their drawings or written words as they feel comfortable. Allow a few moments for youth to react aloud to the words of prophecy they've heard.

Connecting to the Story (10–15 minutes)
OPTION A
Needed: "Who Is Like God?" handouts, writing utensils

Give each youth a copy of the "Who Is Like God?" handout. Invite them to find a partner or two (depending on the size of your class) and spend about fifteen minutes working through the handout.

After all of the small groups have finished, invite them back together and have them share the contents of their discussions as much as your time allows. Be sure, however, to have all the small groups share the prayers they wrote at the end of the handout.

Don't lose these prayers. You might choose to use them in an option later in the session. Or you could consider using these in a more public forum, such as by reading them in congregational worship or printing them in the church newsletter. If you have a large class and several prayers, you might even be able to create a small devotional booklet. If you are using this session during the Advent season, you could give the booklet an Advent theme through artwork and other writings. Given the time, this could be a valuable activity for your class members, even using desktop publishing or Web design software, if that's available to you. If you make these prayers public in any way, be sure to get the class's permission.

OPTION B
Needed: poster board, glue, markers, news papers, news magazines
Make poster board, glue, markers, newspapers, and news magazines available to the group. Ask for a volunteer to read Micah 4:3-4 out loud to the group again. After hearing the passage, invite group members to take fifteen minutes to scan

the papers and magazines for headlines and photographs that illustrate parts of the verse, tearing them out and gluing them to the poster board collage-style. (If you have a smaller class—say, three to five people—you might work on a single collage for the class. Larger classes might be broken into smaller groups, each creating its own collage. If you have enough materials, you could even have each youth create his or her own individual collage.) Class members might also use the markers to write or draw on the collage. The collages might take the focus of where God's peace is needed, or they might focus, instead, on where peace is occurring.

After they've created their collages, invite them to write a prayer on their collage, asking for God's help in making peace.

Exploring the Story (10–15 minutes)

OPTION A

Needed: "What's Going On?" handouts, Bible study helps, writing utensils

In this option, class members will explore more of the historical background to the Micah passage. Make available Bible study resources, such as atlases, commentaries, encyclopedias, and dictionaries. Give the class members each a copy of the "What's Going On?" handout. Instruct them to get into pairs and work through their handouts together, discovering more about the setting in which this prophecy is offered. At the end of the handout, they are invited to consider current events that might match, in some ways, those they will discover in the setting of the biblical passage. In your instructions to the group, you might have them recall some of their findings from "Connecting to the Story" at that point, particularly if you did Option B above. Many of the things they found for the collages might well illustrate their discussions in this option now.

OPTION B

Needed: Bibles

Begin this step by having youth brainstorm various rallying cries they might remember or have learned about from history. An obvious example is "Remember the Alamo!" Ask:
■ What is a phrase like that supposed to accomplish?
■ If a general were addressing an army, what might he or she be trying to get them to do, feel, or think about by saying, "Remember the Alamo"?

Now, have the group read together Joel 3:9-10. This passage is rather shocking, after having read its reverse in Micah. Inform the class that many Bible scholars think that the Joel saying might be older. These scholars also think it might stem from a common rallying cry similar to "Remember the Alamo!" It might have been a saying that ancient kings used to get their people to emotionally gird up for battle. Ask:
■ If that's so, how do you think people who heard Micah's prophecy would have reacted to Micah's reversal of the words?
■ How might it sound to us today to say something like "It's time to forget the Alamo, and put it behind us"?

If you brainstormed other rallying cries together as a class, take a few moments to put them in reverse. Next, have volunteers read Psalm 46:9, Psalm 76:3, Isaiah 2:2-4 (almost identical to Micah), John 14:27, and Galatians 3:28. Discuss:

■ What are the differences among these passages, if any?

■ Who is the subject of the passage? In other words, who's doing the peacemaking in the passage (it may not be obvious)?

■ If we take all the passages together, what might that teach us about peace?

Living the Story (5–10 minutes)

OPTION A

Needed: Bibles, hymnals or songbooks (optional), paper, writing utensils

Bible scholars generally agree that much of Micah was put into written form in a way intended to be used in public worship settings. Many of the passages have the feel of a litany response between a leader and the people. Perhaps Micah 4:1-5 was designed so that a leader could speak the first four verses and then the people could respond by speaking the fifth verse. (For the purposes of this step, we will be leaving off the last three verses of today's Scripture passage. You may choose to include them, but verse 5 provides a wonderful closure to the session.)

As a group, create a brief worship service that will encompass the learnings of the entire session. Keep in mind that verse 5 is actually a call to commitment, a challenge to act in a particular way. Spend a few minutes discussing what that challenge is, and invite the youth to make a personal commitment of some sort to how God is calling them to "walk the walk" in their own particular situations. In creating your worship experience, use Micah 4:1-5 as a litany, and incorporate any other prayers the class may have created during the session, other Scripture readings, and any related songs or hymns the class chooses. They may also choose to share their commitments or create a way to celebrate commitments as a part of the worship. Either use the worship as your closing experience or make arrangements to use it as a congregational experience.

OPTION B

Needed: banner-making materials, such as fabric, scissors, glue, and decorative elements

Today's passage contains many wonderful visual images. For this option, the class will create a banner to illustrate the passage and their learnings from the session. If you do not feel artistically talented, this is a perfect opportunity to have someone from the congregation work with the youth to create the banner. Make arrangements ahead of time to hang the completed banner someplace where the whole congregation could enjoy it. Make sure the youth consider the content of their discussions and study as they make the banner, and be sure all the youth are included in the banner-making process in some way.

Things to Ponder

Today's youth are very concerned about issues of peace and justice, including human and environmental justice. Their concerns might take a different shape than did the protests of the 1960s, but they are no less idealistic and hopeful. On the other hand, today's youth tend to have cynicism mixed in with their idealism. Discussions of the hope expressed in Micah will bring out this mix. If the youth make particular commitments to peacemaking activities as a part of the session's plan, be sure to find ways to follow up and support those commitments.

Looking Ahead

Be sure to read through the options for the next session far enough in advance that you can gather the supplies needed. There are no unusual supplies required, but some of the steps may require a little advance preparation. For example, you will need to recruit youth in your group to assist you in Option B of both "Setting the Stage" and "Telling the Story."

Who Is Like God?

The name Micah means, in Hebrew, "Who is like Yahweh?" You might already know that Yahweh is the Hebrew name for God. Micah, then, was a prophet whose very name bore the intention of getting the people around him to think about what it meant to be God's people, to pattern their lives after what God would want them to be.

1. Read Micah 4:1-2.

2. Brainstorm for a moment or two, as a small group, what kinds of things might be included in God's "paths." What might be important to God? List these things on the back of this handout. (Be sure to leave plenty of room—you have lots of things to write on the back of this page!)

3. After you've got a few things on your list, read the following passages and see what they have to say about what it means to follow God's paths. Using these passages, add to your list words and phrases that describe the kinds of things that might be included in God's paths.

Micah 6:8   Exodus 20:1-17   Matthew 5:1-12
Matthew 7:12   Mark 12:28-34   John 13:34-35

4. If words and attitudes could be considered "weapons of war," what kinds of things do you see happening in your school, among your friends, in your church, in your community, or in the world that could be this kind of warfare? List some of those things on the back of this handout as well.

5. The New Revised Standard Version of the Bible translates Micah 4:3b as saying that "nation shall not lift up sword against nation, neither shall they learn war any more." What does it mean to "learn" war? What might that mean in respect to your discussion of question 4, about words and attitudes?

6. If your name meant "Who is like God?" how would you try to live your life, given the things this Scripture passage says?

7. As a group, write a three- or four-sentence prayer to God about the things you've discussed on this handout.

What's Going On?

What you'll need: commentaries, Bible dictionaries and/or encyclopedias, atlases, or other similar study helps.

Read through the following information on the historical background to Micah 4:1-8 and then do as many of the activities suggested as you have resources available. (Only the first two steps are dependent on having study resources; the rest you may do with your Bibles and your brains!)

1. Read Micah 1:1, and using a Bible dictionary or encyclopedia, look up the names of some of the kings mentioned in that verse. If Micah is associated with these kings, then at about what time was the prophet Micah active?

2. Look up Moresheth, the town in which Micah lived. What kind of town was it? Can you locate it on a map of the ancient world? (You may or may not be able to, depending on the map.)

3. Micah lived in a particular time of Israel's history. During this time, the Hebrew people were divided into two kingdoms: Israel and Judah. Micah lived in Judah. Read the following passages to find out some of what was happening in Israel and Judah at the same time that Micah was prophesying: 2 Kings 16:1-9 (King Ahaz of Judah strikes a deal with Assyria and begins to pay tribute); 2 Kings 17:1-20 (King Hoshea of Israel causes Israel to be invaded by Assyria; Israel is conquered; Judah also turns from following God); 2 Kings 17:21-23 (Israel is exiled in Jeroboam's reign); 2 Chronicles 32 (skim the chapter—this is Hezekiah's reign).

4. During the time of siege and warfare all around, the common people, the poor people of the towns and countryside, would have fared badly. The northern kingdom of Israel was conquered by Assyria in 722 BCE. Judah avoided being conquered, but in order to do so, it paid huge tribute (or taxes) to the kingdom of Assyria. These taxes (in money and food) would have come from the backbreaking labor of the common people of Judah. In addition, at the same time that Judah was paying tribute, it was also pouring tremendous money and effort into building up armies and creating weaponry. Finally, Judah's traditions and religious practices were being diffused by efforts to accommodate another nation's practices. The Judean kings began to worship other gods than Yahweh. Micah blamed the leaders for the struggles of the poor. Read Micah 4:1-5 again—what is Micah saying here, given the situation he and his fellow Judeans were living in? (If you have access to Bible encyclopedias or commentaries, take a few minutes to do a little more research into the historical situation at the time.)

5. Today, are there any situations comparable to the kinds of things Micah is saying? For example, discuss the difference between a country spending money to help feed its people versus spending money on weapons and armies (verse 3). Does this ever happen? When and where? What would Micah have to say about it?

6. Rewrite Micah 4:1-8 as if Micah were prophesying today. To whom would Micah be talking? What situations would he address? How would the prophesy be worded?

4. The Greatest among You

Bible Story: Matthew 20:20-28

Paul Mast-Hewitt

A Story behind the Story

This brief account of the two brothers' request occurs in the context of Jesus' final journey to Jerusalem, where he would be arrested, tried, and killed. Yet it seems that at least some of the disciples must have expected something different upon arriving in Jerusalem. Perhaps they expected Jesus to finally be revealed as the messianic king.

Only a few short verses earlier, Jesus told the disciples that one day the Son of Man would be seated on a throne and that they, the disciples, would also be seated on twelve thrones, "judging the twelve tribes of Israel" (Matthew 19:28). Never mind that in Matthew's story Jesus had also just revealed his expectation of being arrested and killed upon arrival in Jerusalem. It seems far more likely that the sons of Zebedee (James and John) were still pondering the twelve thrones when they had their mother ask for them to be seated at Jesus' right and left hands. (Having their mother make the request would have been considered more polite than being so crass as to make the request themselves.)

Jesus then asked if they would be able to drink the cup that he would drink. It seems clear in retrospect that this refers to his suffering and death, especially when read alongside Matthew 20:28. Yet James and John probably didn't fully get it. One's "cup" could refer to one's lot in life—blessings and sufferings (see Psalm 23:5 or Ezekiel 23:31-33). What did James and John think Jesus meant? We may never know for sure, but apparently they believed they were able to drink it.

It seems the disciples still didn't understand. Jesus gathered the rest of the disciples (who were indignant at the brothers) and repeated a lesson of the kingdom. Only two short chapters earlier (in Matthew 18:1-5), the disciples asked Jesus, "Who is the greatest in the kingdom of heaven?" Jesus responded by bringing a child into the inner circle. This time he repeated the theme, turning the world's priorities upside down. Surely a slave was about as opposite as possible from ruler, and who thinks of servants as great?

Enter the Story

Take a few minutes to find a quiet place with few distractions. Be sure to bring paper and pen to record your thoughts. Read through the story again. Reflect on your own life as you let the words of Scripture sink in. Jot down any thoughts that come to mind. You might want to consider these questions:

- What question do I have to bring to Jesus?
- How might Jesus respond to my question?
- How can I seek to serve the learners in the class this week?

Setting the Stage
(5–10 minutes)
OPTION A
Needed: Reserved signs
Before the lesson, make two large signs that say *Reserved*. Place them on the two most preferred seats in the classroom before anybody arrives. As the students arrive, greet them as you do normally. If anybody asks about the reserved seats, insist that no one sit there, because they are reserved. After everyone has arrived and found a place to sit, hopefully one slightly different from their usual one, ask how they felt about not being able to sit in the favorite spots.

If your room does not have comfortable seats that are in higher demand than the others, you could stir things up a little by arriving early and sitting in a completely different place than usual—perhaps in the back of the room or in somebody else's regular spot. Then you can talk about what's the best seat for the leader and why that would be the best spot. Explain that today's story has to do with preferred seating.

OPTION B
Needed: two youth volunteers
Long before the lesson, recruit one or two key people in the group to dramatize this story. Think of something that a lot of people in your group would really like but for which nobody has the gall to ask you. It could be permission to leave early, the keys to your car, etc. Instruct your co-conspirators to ask you for that prized something at an agreed-upon signal from you at the beginning of the class session. The signal should be something that won't be obvious to the rest of the group, such as when you shut the door to begin class.

When everybody has arrived and you are ready to begin class, casually give the signal. At that point your co-conspirators should approach you to ask for that special perk. Act surprised and then, after an appropriate pause that will make everyone wonder if you'll give in, give an obtuse answer like "So, *you* think you can drive *my* car." Play it up as much as you like, but be careful not to embarrass your assistants too much. Have them return to their seats, and thank them for their help.

Discuss how it feels when someone might get something special that the rest of the group might also like to have. Explain that the story for today is about just such a request made by two of the disciples.

Telling the Story
(5–10 minutes)
OPTION A
Needed: Bible
Tell the youth that you are going to read the story for today and that it may contain statements that are surprising. When they hear something that seems contrary to common sense, they are to make an *oooooh* or an *aaaaah* sound (like they're aghast). Practice the sounds a couple of times. You may have to exaggerate the sound at this point so the learners feel more comfortable making such a silly sound. Then read the passage as you normally would.

POSSIBLE YOUTH CONTACT POINTS
- Who are the most important people?
- What does it mean to be a great person?
- Why do I just not get it sometimes?
- How are we to live as Christians?
- What's important to God?

YOU MAY NEED
- two signs that say *Reserved*
- Bibles
- "Readers' Theater" handouts (six copies)
- paper and pens or pencils
- newsprint or dry-erase board and markers, or chalkboard and chalk
- four pieces of newsprint labeled with the names of the characters
- blank paper
- "What It Means to Me" handouts
- Bible study aids, such as commentaries, dictionaries, concordances, etc.
- markers and crayons

Go ahead and have fun with this step, but make sure the youth understand that they are to make their responses only at something that is contrary to common sense.

OPTION B
Needed: "Readers' Theater" handouts, youth assistants as readers
Before the session, recruit youth to be the following characters: narrator, Jesus, mother of the sons of Zebedee, and the two sons of Zebedee. (If you have fewer than five students, you can take one or more of the roles, and everyone together can take the part of the other disciples.) Give them copies of the "Readers' Theater" with their parts highlighted the week before so they can become familiar with their lines. You might want to gather before the class to read through it together a couple of times as well.

Then, when it is time for the telling of the story, have the characters come forward and introduce them to the rest of the class. Explain to the rest of the class that they also have a part. They are to be the other disciples. Have them practice their part by saying, "Oooooh!" (The tone is to be that of a child who sees another child do something wrong, as in, "Oooooh! You're gonna be in trooouuuble!") Now everybody is ready to begin. Have the characters take their places and read through the script. Afterward, thank everybody for their role and have them sit down again.

Reacting to the Story (10–15 minutes)
OPTION A
Needed: newsprint or dry-erase board and markers, or chalkboard and chalk
Have the board or easel ready with appropriate writing utensils. Invite one youth to act as recorder, writing the responses of the group to the discussion questions onto the newsprint, dry-erase board, or chalkboard. Invite the class to consider what surprised them most in the story or what jumps out at them about the story. If you used Option A of "Telling the Story," you could ask what caused them to say, "Oooooh" or "Aaaaah." Why are those things surprising, or what makes them stand out?

OPTION B
Needed: newsprint labeled with the names of the characters, markers, tape
Before the class, label four pieces of newsprint with the names of the characters: the mother of the sons of Zebedee, the brothers, Jesus, the ten disciples. Post these on the walls of the room, slightly spread out. Have numerous markers available.

Invite the learners to go to the four pieces of newsprint and write how they think that character may have felt in this story. They can write a single word or a phrase to describe the feelings of the characters. If they are more artistically inclined, they may draw a simple face with an expression that matches what they think the character(s) might have been feeling during the story. After they have written or drawn something for each of the characters, they can return to their seats. If time allows, you can read through the lists of emotions.

Connecting to the Story (10–15 minutes)

OPTION A

Needed: Bibles, paper, writing utensils

Hand out paper and a writing utensil to each youth. Explain that much of the imagery in the story was contemporary two thousand years ago, but society has changed a great deal since then and some of the imagery is no longer current. Explain to the youth that they are to modernize the story by substituting imagery that fits our modern world. This might mean just changing a word in one place, but it might require a reworking of a whole paragraph in another place. Explain that this is to help them understand the story better. Again, if there are those who enjoy drawing, encourage them to illustrate their stories or to create it as a cartoon-style storyboard or mural.

After the learners have had a few minutes to write, ask for a couple of volunteers to read their modernized stories.

OPTION B

Needed: "What It Means to Me" handouts, writing utensils

Give each learner a copy of the "What It Means to Me" handout and a writing utensil. Explain that they are going to write what some of the more out-of-date imagery

means to them. To define the phrasing, they might want to think of new imagery that might replace it in today's world. Explain that they will have a chance to do the second part of the handout later in the lesson. If time allows, you might have some of the learners share their definitions.

Exploring the Story (10–15 minutes)

You might want to break into two subgroups and have each group do one of the options below. At the end of the work, the groups could teach each other the material that they have learned.

OPTION A

Needed: Bibles, paper, writing utensils

In this activity the learners will explore a little more of the context of this story in Matthew. Form groups of three to five learners (if your group is small, they can all work together). Hand out paper and a pencil to each group and have them choose a scribe and a reporter. The scribe will record the work of the group on the paper. Then, when all the groups have had time to work, the reporter will tell the other groups what his or her group learned.

Explain that they are going to look up a passage in Matthew that occurred before the story you read earlier. They are to read that story and ask the question "What does this have to do with the story about the sons of Zebedee?" Other questions they might want to consider include these:

- How might this episode have affected the feelings of the characters in today's story?
- What might the characters have been thinking about in today's story?

Have half of the group(s) look up Matthew 18:1-4 and the other half look up Matthew 19:27-30. If you want, you could have three different passages and have some of the learners look up Matthew 20:17-19. When everybody has had time to work (after about five minutes), ask the reporters to share their groups' findings.

OPTION B

Needed: "What It Means to Me" handouts, writing utensils, Bible study aids

This can be used to follow up on Option B of "Connecting to the Story," or it can be a stand-alone activity. If you did not use the handouts in the previous activity, you might want to write the phrases listed on the handouts on an easel so everyone can see them. Explain to the youth that they are going to be trying to find some expert opinions on what these phrases might have meant. Tell them they can work in groups of three to five people. Using the Bible study aids, they are to find information that will help them define these phrases.

Obviously, they will not be able to look up the phrases directly. They can look up individual words in the Bible dictionaries and concordances, or they might find clues in commentaries. The learners can individually record their discoveries on the back of the handout (or write them on blank paper, if the handout was not used).

Living the Story
(5–10 minutes)
OPTION A

Needed: paper, markers or crayons

As you hand out the paper, tell the youth that they will be able to take this home after today's lesson to use for further reflection. In fact, you might want to encourage them to find a journal they might use for ongoing spiritual reflection. To give them a feel for doing this type of reflection, ask the youth to consider everything they've done in this session, from beginning to end. Invite them to think about their impressions of the Scripture when it was first read versus their impressions of the Scripture story now, after they've spent some time with it. Offer the learners use of pens, markers, and crayons and instruct them to use the paper to write or draw something that reflects what they have learned today.

After a suitable amount of time, close the group with prayer.

OPTION B

Needed: "What It Means to Me" handouts, pencils

This can be done as follow-up to Option B of "Connecting to the Story" whether or not the handout was also used for Option B of "Exploring the Story." Have the learners look at the definitions for the phrases they wrote earlier. Ask them to make any changes they would like to based on what they may have learned in "Exploring the Story." Then have them complete the last two parts of the handout, summarizing the point or points of the passage and answering the question "What does this story mean for your life?" If time allows, ask for volunteers to share their answers to this last question.

Close with a prayer asking God to help your group live out the teachings of Jesus, possibly incorporating some of what was shared from the last question on the handout. Be sure to do so in a way that won't embarrass anybody.

Things to Ponder

This story can really challenge our priorities and values. Some of the youth may catch the radical reversal of values that Jesus advocates in this story and may feel the need to make changes in their personal lives. Others may see hypocrisy among Christians who do not live these values. It is important to address these responses directly. The question of hypocrisy can be addressed by talking about the need to focus on our own behaviors—that is the arena in which we can make changes. For those who accept the challenge to make changes, try to provide concrete help in implementing those changes.

Looking Ahead

Depending on which options you choose, you may need to locate a copy of the video called *The Visual Bible: Matthew* and cue it to the appropriate place. Another option suggests using a recording of U2's song "When I Look at the World." You may also need to obtain a copy of the book called *The Prayer of Jabez*. Specific suggestions for obtaining these resources are offered in "You May Need" and in the options themselves. Finally, one of the options suggests inviting a special guest into your classroom. If you choose this option, you will need to find someone who fits the description and then invite him or her to participate ahead of time.

Readers' Theater

Matthew 20:20-28

Cast: Narrator
Mother of the sons of Zebedee
Sons of Zebedee (2)
Jesus
Other disciples (the audience)

Jesus stands alone at center stage, while the sons of Zebedee and their mother stand just off stage. Characters are then to follow the action that is indicated by the narration.

Narrator: The mother of the sons of Zebedee came to him with her sons, and kneeling before him, she asked a favor of him.

Mother: May I ask you something?

Jesus: What do you want?

Mother: Declare that these two sons of mine will sit, one at your right hand and one at your left, in your kingdom.

Narrator: Turning to her sons, Jesus answered:

Jesus: You do not know what you are asking. Are you able to drink the cup that I am about to drink?

Sons of Zebedee: We are able.

Jesus: You will indeed drink my cup, but to sit at my right hand and at my left, this is not mine to grant, but it is for those for whom it has been prepared by my Father.

Narrator: When the ten heard it, they were angry with the two brothers.

Other disciples: Oooooh! [Like a child might say when somebody else does something wrong]

Narrator: But Jesus called them to him and said,

Jesus: You know that the rulers of the Gentiles lord it over them, and their great ones are tyrants over them. It will not be so among you; but whoever wishes to be great among you must be your servant, and whoever wishes to be first among you must be your slave; just as the Son of Man came not to be served but to serve and to give his life as a ransom for many.

~~~~~~

What It Means to Me

Below are some phrases from the passage. In your own words, explain what these might mean to you. You might want to think of imagery that is more contemporary to help you explain what these mean.

"To sit, one at your right hand and one at your left":

"Drink the cup that I am about to drink":

"Rulers of the Gentiles lord it over them":

"To give his life as a ransom":

Now that you have had a chance to think through some of the phrases, in the space below, write a couple of sentences to summarize the point or points of this story.

What does this story mean for your life?

5. Heart, Soul, and Mind

Bible Story: Matthew 22:34-40

Mark Luera

A Story behind the Story

Consider this fictional journal entry from a first-century male peasant.

Ever since I was taken to the temple on my twelfth birthday, God became more remote instead of closer. It seems so ironic. In the temple I almost saw God. His presence filled the temple, and I knew God was real. Unfortunately, that was the end of my religious education.

But religion is a matter of following the law, not knowing God. There are commands for every occasion—what to do for Sabbath, what to do each month of the year, what to do when you get sick and when you get well. I know all this is important, but I wanted to *see* God! And every time I asked a scribe or Pharisee about that, he would ignore me or tell me to stay in my place. There is such a gap between the teachers and the people.

Then I learned about a man like me. Poor and not educated in the temple, he nevertheless spoke with such authority about God, as if he really knew God.

So I started following him and listening to him right after I saw him come into Jerusalem on a donkey.

He showed authority when he cleansed the temple of the money changers. When the chief priests and elders asked who gave him authority to teach about God, he wouldn't tell them! (See Matthew 21:23-27.) When he told parables about the kingdom of God that left out the leaders of our people, they got very angry. (See Matthew 21:45-46.) But they would do nothing to him because more and more people were following him and listening to him.

And every time the leaders tried to outsmart him in front of the crowds and prove that they knew more than he did, he turned the tables on them! He could answer all their questions and make them look stupid. (See Matthew 22:15-33.)

Then they tried to embarrass him by asking him to sum up the whole law in just one commandment. He said, "If you want to understand all the Law and the Prophets, just remember two things, which are of equal importance: Love God and love your neighbor." (See Matthew 22:34-40.) They were stunned!

Not since the greatest Jew of all—Moses—had anyone spoken with such authority. That's when I knew I would follow this man all the days of my life, for I was seeing God.

Enter the Story

People like summaries—"bottom line" statements. We want to know that "it all boils down to this. . . ." Of course, such summaries can too easily simplify the complexity of truths and doctrines and rituals that make up a religious tradition. So the Pharisees thought they might trap Jesus into sounding ridiculous by trying to sum up the whole law! What is your "bottom line" statement when it comes to Christian faith? How does that simple statement help you live a Christian lifestyle? In what ways might your summary statement hinder you from living a Christian lifestyle? Consider these questions as you read through Matthew 22:34-40.

Setting the Stage (5–10 minutes)

OPTION A

As the learners gather, engage their attention with what is known as a "forced choice continuum." Explain the activity by saying, *This side of the room is Choice A. The other side of the room is Choice B. Stand on a side of the room according to the choice with which you most identify in the following.* After reading a choice, give the youth a minute or so to go to the side of the room they've chosen; no one may stand in the middle.

Call on a person or two to explain why he or she made that choice after each statement. Say: *Are you more . . . ?*

- caramel or chocolate?
- high or low?
- country or city?
- coin or paper bill?
- romance novel or science fiction novel?
- SUV or sports car?
- flower or tree?
- pickup truck or limousine?

Make up your own forced choices to supplement or replace these.

After you've had some fun with the exercise, explain to the youth that sometimes we are forced to make choices much more important than these, even about our faith or our identities. If you've got time, consider having a brief discussion about the difficulties in making

decisions from so many choices available to us.

OPTION B

Needed: newsprint and markers or chalkboard and chalk, paper, writing utensils

On newsprint or chalkboard, have the group list five or six movies and books that everyone has seen or read. Give each participant paper and a writing utensil and ask them to write a one-sentence summary of each item on the list. The sentences should not be over twenty words long. Students should work quietly by themselves.

After you call time, invite one person to read her or his summation of the first work. Write it on newsprint or chalkboard. Allow the rest of the group to critique the summary statement. How different or similar were their summaries? Debate the relative merits of different summaries, trying to reach a consensus as to which statement is the best summary. Repeat this process for each item on the list.

After you've taken a stab at it, discuss with the group the difficulties of summarizing. Often what seems important to one person is a minor thing to someone else. Point out to the group that it is difficult for Christians to agree on how to summarize what faith is all about.

Telling the Story (5–10 minutes)

OPTION A

Needed: "The Back Story" handouts, two volunteers, Bibles, straight-backed chair (optional)

Prepare to tell the story from the perspective of the conflict between

POSSIBLE YOUTH CONTACT POINTS

- Am I willing to experience controversy for the sake of the gospel?
- Which is more important to faith: knowledge or lifestyle?
- What does it mean for me to love my neighbor?
- What is love?

YOU MAY NEED

- Bibles
- newsprint or chalkboard
- markers or chalk
- writing paper
- pencils or pens
- "The Back Story" handouts (two copies)
- straight-backed chair (optional)
- "Names for God" handouts
- *The Visual Bible: Matthew* (Visual Entertainment Disc: 1998, ISBN: 1889710008), generally available at Christian bookstores and at amazon.com, or check your local Christian resource borrowing library
- TV and VCR
- copies of Matthew 22:34-40 from the New International Version of the Bible
- recording of U2's "When I Look at the World" (on CD entitled *All That You Can't Leave Behind*)
- CD player
- copies of the lyrics to the above U2 song (one per person)
- Polaroid, video, or digital camera, tape recorder, or other visual or audio recording devices (all optional)
- Bible concordances (if available)
- visitor, as described in Option A of "Living the Story"
- *The Prayer of Jabez: Breaking through to a Blessed Life* by Bruce Wilkinson (optional)

the Sadducees and the Pharisees ("The Back Story" handout). These two groups often vehemently disagreed with each other, but both of these parties were aggravated by the popularity of Jesus. So both groups sought to discredit him in the eyes of the crowds who followed him. They also both wanted to show his unworthiness as a teacher in comparison to themselves. The Pharisees, especially, enjoyed debate, constantly arguing over points of law. Most of Matthew 22 (verses 15-46) is given over to this contest.

Assign the parts of the Sadducee and the Pharisee to two of the learners ahead of time. Let them read over their part on the handout. Also, assign someone to read Matthew 22:34-40. The person who is the Sadducee should read first, then the Pharisee, and finally the reader of the Scripture should follow. To make the hearing of the passage a little unusual, have the readers take turns sitting in a straight-backed chair while the listeners stand in front of them.

OPTION B

Needed: TV and VCR, **The Visual Bible: Matthew** *(cued to Matthew 22:34)*

Watch together the excerpt from the *Visual Bible* that includes Matthew 22:34-40. (This video of the Gospel of Matthew was shot on location in Morocco and South Africa, which makes for a Middle Eastern–looking setting. The script is taken strictly from the New International Version of the Bible in an attempt to be faithful to the Scripture. Scripture references are printed in the video frame so that

you can easily begin at Matthew 22:34 and end at Matthew 22:40. Ask your denominational resource library for a rental copy or purchase the four videocassettes for Matthew from a Christian bookstore.) Pass around a bowl of popcorn while your youth watch!

Afterward, look at the passage from the New Revised Standard Version and compare it to the New International Version. Are there any differences significant enough to have affected the way the scene was filmed? Is a visual translation of the Bible helpful for getting in touch with what really happened, or does a movie add too many interpretations to the bare biblical text? Feel free to take a few moments to discuss with the group how a visual experience of the Scripture may help or hinder one's understanding and interpretation of it.

Reacting to the Story (15–20 minutes)

OPTION A

Needed: paper, writing utensils, newsprint, markers

Hand out blank pieces of paper and writing utensils, and invite the group to write a list of questions that they would like Jesus to answer. These can be based on the Scripture story or just be questions in general.

Let the group know that you're going to hold a press conference. Choose someone to be Jesus, or it might be helpful to ask a guest to attend this session—someone who is well versed in Scripture—and ask him to play Jesus. Everyone else can be reporters who are trying to get a story. The reporters should vie for

Jesus' attention just like in White House press conferences. When someone is called upon, everyone else should be quiet. Reporters can try to ask follow-up questions. To the best of his ability, Jesus should try to give scriptural answers. As can be seen from Matthew 22:23-27, the real Jesus didn't always answer the question or give straightforward answers. Let the press conference develop as the participants take it. When it seems to have run out of steam, call time.

Write on newsprint those questions that most perplexed Jesus in the skit. Ask the group if they have any responses to those questions, then suggest the youth seek the answers to those questions in the weeks to come. Invite them to consult with ministers, church leaders, and respected teachers.

OPTION B
(This option will best follow Option A of "Telling the Story," but it may be used in either case.)
Needed: Bibles
Tell the students that Jesus often surprised and amazed people in his responses to tricky or troubling questions or in his parables. Ask questions like the following:
■ What, if anything, do you find surprising about Jesus' statements in the passage?
■ Does the element of surprise or amazement seem more pronounced when you know something about the Sadducees and Pharisees? (See Option A, "Telling the Story.")
Hand out blank paper and writing utensils to the students. Invite them to draw three columns on their papers, labeled "Heart,"
"Soul," and "Mind." Say something like this: *In the appropriate column, write things or people or events that most occupy your heart, soul, or mind.* For instance, in the heart column, they might write "family" or "boyfriend" (or "girl-friend"). In the mind column, they might write, "How to pass geometry." In the soul column, they might write, "Figuring out how to sleep late on Sunday instead of going to Sunday school."

After they've followed your directions, have them get into pairs to discuss the following questions:
■ Where in your life do you make room for God?
■ Does the answer surprise you? Why or why not?
■ How might you make more room for God in your life?

Connecting to the Story (15–20 minutes)
OPTION A
Needed: CD player, U2 CD All That You Can't Leave Behind cued to "When I Look at the World," copies of lyrics, newsprint and markers or chalkboard and chalk
Remind the students that the Jewish leaders and teachers, as represented in Matthew's Gospel, had a difficult time seeing the world as Jesus saw it. Do we have an easier time?

Listen to the song "When I Look at the World" from the album *All That You Can't Leave Behind* by U2. The song tells about the difficulties of seeing reality as Jesus sees it—with complete love and grace. But the singer wants to learn to see and act as Jesus does.

Invite people to sit comfortably and close their eyes as they listen.

After they've listened once, give them the lyrics in print and ask them to read through them quietly. Encourage the students to simply respond to the song—from its musical style to its lyrics. Ask:
■ In what ways does it describe your own faith dilemmas?
■ How can we see through the eyes of Jesus if we don't know much about him?
■ What is essential for us to know about Jesus?

Consider writing responses on newsprint or chalkboard. Add Scripture references to your list if you can.

OPTION B
Needed: Polaroid, video, or digital camera, tape recorder, or other visual or audio recording devices (all optional)
To further explore the ideas of seeing the world though the eyes of Jesus, engage the group in a video project. You can make this as sophisticated or as simple as your resources and expertise allow, either simply doing a photo collage or producing a full-out computer-edited digital video.

To start, ask the group to brainstorm what they might do with the theme "Seeing the World through Jesus' Eyes" or "Loving God with All Your Heart, Soul, and Mind." They may come up with a certain story line or conduct interviews or record an event or tape a segment on life on the streets. Have the group formulate the plan and make assignments, but you should make sure everyone is involved in some way.

Help them make whatever arrangements they will need, and think about the audience to whom you might present the finished project. Perhaps it could be included in congregational worship at some point.

Exploring the Story (15–20 minutes)
OPTION A
Needed: "Names for God" handouts, Bibles, writing utensils
Begin by having the youth read the handout "Names for God." If you have a large group, you could break into smaller groups, assigning Scriptures from section 1, 2, or 3 to each group to study and prepare a report for the whole class. If you prefer to work as a single group, choose just a few Scriptures from sections 1, 2, and 3 on which to concentrate.

Whether you make assignments or work as a group, begin developing a list of names and attributes for God. Write these on newsprint or chalkboard along with the Scripture reference from which it comes. Ask the group to respond to the following:
■ What experiences of God have you had that add to the biblical names or attributes of God?
■ How important are these experiences?
■ When you pray, how do you address God?
■ How do others you know address God in prayer?

Invite each student to write a brief prayer using a name that he or she has never before used for God. Then encourage them to get together in pairs and pray their prayers together.

OPTION B

Needed: Bible concordances (if available), Bibles, paper, writing utensils

Engage the learners in a scriptural exploration of the concept of a "neighbor." Have the youth use a concordance to find references to "neighbor" throughout the Bible. (You might want to break into pairs or triads for this activity.) If they seem to be stuck, or if you don't have a concordance, ask the learners to look at the following passages: Exodus 20:16-17; 22:1-28; Leviticus 19:9-18; 25:13-17; Deuteronomy 5:20-21; 15:2-3,7,9, 11-12; 19:14; 22:1-4; Psalm 28:3; 101:5; Proverbs 3:28; Jeremiah 34:17; Matthew 19:19; Mark 12:31,33; Luke 10:27; 15:9; Romans 13:9; Galatians 5:14; and James 2:8.

Hand out paper and invite the youth to draw four columns on it. They should label the columns "Scripture Passage," "How to Treat a Neighbor," "Consequences for Ill Treatment of a Neighbor," and "Comments." As they read the Scripture passages, they should note each passage in the first column, then write words and phrases from the Scripture in the second and third columns as appropriate. Invite them to use the last column to write questions, insights, connections to their own lives, etc.

Discuss the importance of the concept of "neighbor" for biblical faith by asking questions such as, *Why is neighborliness important to Jesus? What does neighborliness have to do with justice, if anything?*

Living the Story (5–10 minutes)

OPTION A

Needed: a visitor

Invite a "neighbor" to visit your group. Choose someone with whom your youth might not ordinarily come in contact and who is open to entering into a relationship with your group. Such a "neighbor" might be a Muslim or Jewish person, a handicapped person, a recovering addict, or anyone else who might help stretch the students' concept of who a neighbor is.

Ask this neighbor to tell the group about himself or herself and the challenges the neighbor must face. Let group members ask questions they may have about this neighbor's lifestyle and ideas about living in the community. Ask, "How can we be loving to this neighbor?" The neighbor may ask for something from the youth or might discuss the appropriateness of their suggestions.

After you have thanked the visitor for participating, challenge the youth to make a commitment to neighborliness by choosing a particular person or group of people and reaching out to them in some specific way. This might be a follow-up to the previous conversation, or they might come up with something unrelated. Invite the youth to make specific plans for this neighborliness, making appropriate assignments, etc. Confirm a time when they will report how this went to the group. Close in prayer, asking God's guidance in being loving to all.

OPTION B

Needed: **The Prayer of Jabez (*if available*), Bibles**

To further encourage youth to see the world through Jesus' eyes, compare *The Prayer of Jabez* to today's Scripture passage. This book, by Bruce Wilkinson, has sold around 5 million copies. The book is based on 1 Chronicles 4:9-10, which mentions an obscure fellow named Jabez who asked God to bless him, to enlarge his borders, and to keep him from harm. (Some biblical translations indicate that his parents prayed this prayer.)

Wilkinson says, "Why not make it a life commitment to ask God every day to bless you—and while he's at it, bless you a lot?"[1]

One critic of this book said, "[Wilkinson] promulgates an American, capitalist definition of blessing, large numbers, and prosperity. Where does that leave Jesus?"[2]

Read 1 Chronicles 4:9-10. Ask the youth: *Do you think this is the way Jesus saw God? Why or why not?* Compare the prayer to Matthew 22:34-40. Ask: *In what ways are or aren't these two passages and perspectives compatible?* Close with a time of prayer, asking God to help you in your faith.

Things to Ponder

This session could take your group away from the church building and into the community. Usually youth are eager to get out and mingle with others if they feel safe and comfortable, so you will want to make sure that they feel secure. That does not mean, though, that you shouldn't encourage youth to step outside their comfort zone—for instance, as they interact with "neighbors" that they had not really had an opportunity to know. Be prepared to follow up with youth after the session.

Looking Ahead

Depending on which options you choose, you may need to compile or obtain a list of inactive youth in your congregation, along with their addresses. You will also need to purchase stamps for these same options. You may also need to compile information on peer mediation, conflict resolution, and peer counseling. Suggestions for potential resources are made in the appropriate options.

Notes

1. Bruce Wilkinson, *The Prayer of Jabez: Breaking through to a Blessed Life* (Sisters, Ore.: Multnomah, 2000), p. 29.
2. Mike Gunn, "Have You Read Jabez Yet?" *Leadership,* summer 2001, p. 12.

~~~~~

The Back Story

The Sadducee
(Based on Matthew 22:23-33)

I am one of an elite class of Jews who managed to maintain their wealth and power during the occupation of our country by the Romans. Thanks to us, the traditions of our faith and our beloved temple and its rituals survived. We kept order among our people for the Romans, and they let us live in the ways of our forefathers.

We kept a tight rein on our people. This was not easy, since we had to constantly deal with the crazy ideas of the Pharisees. We took our stand on what Moses wrote—the first five books of the Bible—and on that alone! There is no evidence of immortality in Moses' writings, nor does he talk about spirits and angels.

When we heard about Jesus preaching to large crowds, we thought he was another Pharisee—somebody who confused the common folk with all kinds of laws and traditions. Since the Pharisees believed in the resurrection of the dead, I assumed Jesus did too. So I thought I'd confuse him with a question about resurrection.

According to Deuteronomy 25:5-10, if a man dies before he and his wife have any children, his brother should marry the widow and raise their first son as if it were the child of the brother who died. (That keeps the family name alive and the family wealth in the family.) So I asked Jesus, "Whose wife would such a woman be in the next life?" Just think—what if she'd had to marry seven brothers because they all kept dying before they had any kids?

Jesus said that the question was irrelevant! In the next life, the old customs and laws don't apply. Then he let me know why he believed in the resurrection of the dead. He said, "If God himself claims to be the God of Abraham and Isaac and Jacob, then they must still be alive, because God isn't God of the dead but of the living."

I have to admit, I hadn't thought of it like that before. I was speechless!

The Pharisees
(Based on Matthew 22:15-22 and Matthew 22:34)

We Pharisees are not tied to temple ritual. We focus our energy on the Torah—the Law. We are determined to bring the Law of Moses to bear on every human act!

We have added many laws on top of it to cover every human act that Moses hadn't thought of. We try to educate the people to know the laws and follow them strictly—this will help them remember always that they are the chosen of God. But this Jesus seemed to disregard the law. We felt he was a dangerous influence.

I decided to set a trap for Jesus by asking, "Is it lawful to pay taxes to the emperor?" What would he say? If he said yes, it would make every Jew mad because we hated paying taxes to the Romans. And besides, one of the Ten Commandments says we should have no other gods before the one true God, but the "god" Caesar is on the Roman coins. However, if Jesus said no, the Romans might hear of it and arrest him for treason.

 Jesus completely outsmarted me, though. He took a coin and asked whose name and image were on it. The crowd shouted, "The emperor's!" Then Jesus said, "So give the emperor the things that are his, and give God the things that are God's." My eyes popped. My face turned red. *It seems so obvious,* I thought as I walked away. *Everything belongs to God!* I wish I'd thought of that first!

Later, some of my friends and I got together to come up with a question that would stump Jesus once and for all. And after that annoying Sadducee got shot down with his question about resurrection, we thought we had our chance . . .

~~~~~

Names for God

Some people find it helpful, when they pray, to call God by a specific name taken from the original language of the Bible. The rich variety of names or references to God in Hebrew has been camouflaged, to some extent, by translating all of them with the one English word "God." The words that get translated so include *El, Elohim, Yahweh, Eloah,* and *Adon* or *Adonai.* In addition, many times *El* was combined with other words to identify God.

For instance, *El-elyon,* translated "the most high God," is found in Genesis 14:18-22, among other places. *El Shaddai,* translated "the Almighty God," can be found in Genesis 17:1. *El Olam,* translated "God the Everlasting One" or "God of Eternity," is found in Genesis 21:33.

The great story of God's self-revelation to Moses includes the divulging of God's name—YHWH (Exodus 3:13-15). This name is used thousands of times throughout the Hebrew Scriptures to refer to God. Today we are uncertain about how to pronounce this name for two reasons: (1) Vowels were not written in ancient Hebrew. Only consonants were written. (2) A tradition developed among the Jews that it was disrespectful to actually say or pronounce the name of God. So the exact pronunciation is lost in history. Christian translators followed in this tradition. Instead of using the name of God revealed to Moses, they substituted the word "Lord" for *Yahweh.*

To further complicate matters, the King James Version of the Bible sometimes translates *Yahweh* as "Jehovah." The King James translators were following an old Jewish combination of letters and vowels. But the Jews had purposely put vowels from *Adonai* with consonants from *Yahweh* to remind themselves not to pronounce the name of God. Therefore, *Jehovah* is an artificial form of the original YHWH.

Many people still use *Jehovah* in combination with other Hebrew words to address God. For instance, *Jehovah-Jireh* (Genesis 22:14, KJV) means "the Lord will provide (or be seen)." *Jehovah-Nissi* (Exodus 17:15, KJV) means "the Lord is my banner." *Jehovah-Shalom* (Judges 6:24, KJV) means "the Lord is peace." To be more accurate, each of these names or attributes of God should be *Yahweh-Jireh, Yahweh-Nissi,* and *Yahweh-Shalom.*

Section 1: Explore other names and references for God by looking at Genesis 49:24; Exodus 34:14; Psalm 18:1-2; Isaiah 30:29; 43:3,14,15; and Habakkuk 1:12.

Section 2: Investigate other descriptions of God in Numbers 23:19; 1 Kings 8:27; Psalm 139:7-12; Isaiah 57:15; and Jeremiah 32:17,27.

Section 3: Check out different titles given to God in Psalm 47:2,7,8; Psalm 96:10; Psalm 121:5; and Isaiah 40:28.

6. Onesimus: More than a Slave
Bible Story: Philemon

Mark Luera

A Story behind the Story

Although this letter raises the issues of slavery and transformation of persons and relationships in Christ, it may also provide an opportunity to reflect on the life and times of Paul. Many times during his work as a missionary for Jesus Christ, Paul was imprisoned. The most extensive imprisonments happened in Caesarea, Ephesus, and Rome.

It seems obvious from Paul's opening remarks that he was literally a prisoner (though a prisoner in the service of the Lord). Since he did not specify where he was imprisoned, however, we can only guess. In fact, we can only guess where Philemon (the one to whom the letter was written) lived. Based on Colossians 4:7-9, it seems probable that Paul's fellow worker Tychicus, accompanied by Onesimus, was on his way to Philemon in Colossae or by way of Colossae.

Other mysteries abound: How did Onesimus become associated with Paul while he was in prison? Had he met Paul when Paul converted Philemon, and did he seek him out for his help, even though Paul himself was a prisoner? As a Roman citizen, Paul had some privileges even while a prisoner. He could have a personal servant, and he could take care of business through personal ambassadors, who could easily visit him in prison.

However their association occurred, Paul obviously was responsible for converting Onesimus to Christ (verse 10) and furthermore had become extremely fond of him (verses 12-13).

Slaves had very limited rights under Roman law. But the law did provide that, when returning a slave, a friend of the master could serve as an advocate on behalf of the slave in the interest of his or her safety and well-being. Perhaps that is why Onesimus came to Paul. Also, freedom was sometimes granted when loyal and deserving slaves reached thirty years of age. Perhaps Onesimus was disappointed that Philemon did not do this and therefore sought out Paul to intercede.

Paul chose to send Onesimus back to Philemon, but everything about their relationship, he felt, should be different because of their common relationship to Jesus Christ.

Enter the Story

In this letter to Philemon, we observe Paul in the ticklish position of playing mediator between a slave (Onesimus) and his master (Philemon). Perhaps you have been in a similar circumstance of playing mediator between two friends or family members. Recall the nature of the dispute and the ways you were able to help, or the frustration you experienced, in trying to bring about reconciliation.

Onesimus apparently wanted to return but needed help in doing so. Have you ever done something that made it difficult to return to a normal relationship? What did you do to "return home" or reenter the good graces of the one you disappointed? Read the story of Philemon and Onesimus with these questions in mind.

Setting the Stage
(5–10 minutes)
OPTION A

Needed: munchies, stamps, stationery, writing utensils, sealing wax and wax stamps, list of addresses of inactive youth

As youth arrive, invite them to sit around a table. Provide munchies of some kind for them to enjoy while they complete a letter. Make the following things available for their use: a variety of stationery and writing implements, interesting first-class stamps, perhaps some sealing wax and wax stamps—whatever you think will help make the letter-writing task more fun. Give them a list of youth who have been absent from church, Sunday school, or youth group. Assign one or two people from the list to each class member. Their goal in writing is to help those peers return to life in your church or group.

Let the participants help one another think of ways to express regret that these friends are no longer active and suggest helpful ways to make them feel welcome again. Avoid guilt-tripping! Invite youth to personalize their letters by recalling something they especially like or miss about the person to whom they are writing.

After the youth have completed their letters, inform them that today's Bible story is actually a letter.

OPTION B

Needed: lengths of rope or yarn, supplies for chosen tasks (as outlined below)

As youth enter the room, pair them up and tie one person's left wrist to another's right wrist. Give pairs a task to accomplish using only the hands that are tied together. Observe how well they work together, and jot down some of your observations. You might set time limits for each task and have the pairs compete to see which pair is fastest.

Possible tasks include lacing up a shoe, tying a bow in a ribbon, filling a cup with water from a pitcher, threading a needle, shuffling a deck of cards, and putting together a simple jigsaw puzzle. Be sure to gather your chosen supplies ahead of time.

Conclude this exercise by sharing your observations about how the pairs worked together. Invite the youth to tell how it felt to be tied together while having to accomplish a task. Did they cooperate effectively with their partner or work at cross-purposes?

The point of the exercise is to start them thinking about how Christians should work together. Ask them to rate (on a scale of 1 to 5) the youth group in terms of its ability to work together. How would the church board rate? Talk about your ratings and why you rated the group(s) the way you did.

Telling the Story
(5–10 minutes)
OPTION A

Needed: Bibles, "Listening Guide" handouts, writing utensils

POSSIBLE YOUTH CONTACT POINTS

- **What is the meaning of friendship?**
- **How does Christian faith change my relationships?**
- **In what ways can Christians work together?**
- **What unity of purpose can I find with other Christians?**
- **What is mediation, and how does it work?**

YOU MAY NEED

- **Bibles**
- **munchies**
- **first-class stamps**
- **stationery**
- **sealing wax and wax stamps (optional)**
- **names and addresses of inactive youth**
- **lengths of rope or yarn**
- **supplies for chosen tasks, such as decks of cards, puzzles, etc. (your options)**
- **"Listening Guide" handouts**
- **"Guidelines for a Discussion about Our Basic Beliefs" handouts**
- **4″ x 6″ index cards**
- **pencils or pens**
- **writing paper**
- **newsprint and markers or chalkboard and chalk**
- **Bible study helps, such as concordances, encyclopedias, dictionaries, etc.**
- **information about mediation, conflict resolution, and peer counseling**

Choose someone in the group to read the Book of Philemon aloud. If possible, this person should read the letter over silently several times first, so that he or she knows how to pronounce any unfamiliar names and understands the gist of the letter.

The reader should divide the reading into four parts, pausing between each part. Verses 1-3 are the opening address. Verses 4-7 are a thanksgiving. Verses 8-21 comprise Paul's request on behalf of Onesimus. And verses 22-25 close the letter with Paul's hopes and additional greetings.

Give each participant a copy of the "Listening Guide" handout and a pencil. As the letter is read, slowly and with pauses between each section, the listeners should jot down their answers to the questions. They will be writing what they hear, so they shouldn't worry about the spelling of proper names. This is more of a "listening guide" than a quiz!

Answers:

1. Paul
2. Prisoner
3. Philemon, Apphia, Archippus, the church in your house
4. Grace and peace
5. Prayer
6. Your love for all the saints; your faith toward Jesus Christ
7. Joy and encouragement
8. Love
9. Onesimus
10. "whose father I have become"; "my own heart"; "I wanted to keep him with me"
11. Slave
12. Beloved brother
13. Paul
14. Paul is the one who converted Philemon
15. "even more than I say"
16. Come visit
17. Epaphras, Mark, Aristarchus, Demas, and Luke

OPTION B
Needed: index cards, writing utensils, Bibles
Divide the group into three subgroups. Give each person an index card. On the top of the index card, those in one subgroup should write "Paul," those in the second subgroup should write "Onesimus," and those in the third subgroup should write "Philemon."

While the Book of Philemon is read aloud, challenge the participants to write down as much information about their character as they can learn from listening. They may stop the reader and ask him or her to repeat the verse just read. They may use their imagination to write down characteristics or descriptions that may only be implied. You may want to read the Scripture twice.

To make this more challenging, give each participant three index cards—one for each of the main characters—and let them try to jot down descriptions of all three while listening.

**Reacting to the Story
(15–20 minutes)**
OPTION A
Needed: "Listening Guide" handouts or index cards from Option B above, newsprint and markers or chalkboard and chalk
If you chose Option A above, engage the participants in a discussion of their answers to the "Listening Guide" handout. You could

simply go around the circle and let each person tell his or her answers to each question in turn, or you could let the group call out answers while you write the correct response on newsprint or chalkboard. Have fun with the spelling of the names in this letter. As you go through the handout, refer to Scripture to settle disputed answers or to clarify answers.

Or if you chose Option B above, invite participants to compare their lists with those of others in their subgroup and come up with a comprehensive list that all in the subgroup agree upon. In the whole group, let a spokesperson for each subgroup write their list on newsprint or chalkboard. The rest of the participants may then challenge specific ideas on the list, asking for clarification or reasoning. Scrutinize especially those ideas that the text might only imply. Refer to the Scripture during this process.

OPTION B

Find two volunteers to role-play the issues in this letter. Invite them to imagine a telephone conversation between two out of the three Scripture characters based on what they know about Paul, Philemon, and Onesimus from this brief letter, filling in the rest with their imaginations. For instance, role-play a phone conversation between Paul and Philemon. Paul might begin by reminiscing with Philemon about how he converted Philemon. He could bring up the subject of Onesimus next. Philemon might interrupt with a few unhappy words about how Onesimus ran away. And so it would go. . . . Continue

the conversation until some resolution is reached.

Find more volunteers for different two-way combinations. A conversation between Paul and Onesimus might proceed along the following lines: Paul expresses surprise that Onesimus has come to see him, wondering where Philemon is. Onesimus then has to tell how he ran away and why. Paul may then give a response based on things he's said in the Scripture story. A conversation between Philemon and Onesimus might begin with some angry words about how Onesimus ran away. Feel free to be imaginative, but encourage the youth to try to be realistic, based on what they know about the characters involved.

Connecting to the Story (15–20 minutes)

OPTION A

Needed: paper, writing utensils, Bibles

Form groups of three or four people. Explain the activity to the youth using words like the following: *From your own experiences and your imaginations, formulate a scenario similar to the one Paul faced. In other words, develop a scenario in which someone mediates a dispute between two estranged friends.* Alternatively, the youth might create a scenario in which someone makes friends with someone from outside his or her usual circle of friends (as Paul made friends with Onesimus). A third option would be to have the learners imagine someone coming to view all of his or her relationships as transformed because of this person's primary relationship to Christ, as Paul suggests to Philemon.

Instruct the groups to write a brief summary of their scenario to convey to the whole group. Explain, *We will choose one of these scenarios to develop into a drama as an entire class.*

Let the whole group choose a particular scenario to develop into a chancel drama that could be used in worship or at a church fellowship dinner to help the whole congregation connect to the letter of Paul to Philemon.

OPTION B
Needed: newsprint and markers or chalkboard and chalk
Remind the class that, among other things, this Scripture story can tell us some things about friendship. Begin by noting on newsprint Paul's references to the relationships he had with Philemon and Onesimus. For instance, in verse 1, Paul referred to Philemon as "our dear friend." Have the youth call out words or phrases from the Scripture that, in some way, define the relationships involved.

Next, ask the learners to reflect on their own friendships by answering the following questions:
■ Which of Paul's terms or phrases seem especially descriptive of your friendships?
■ Which terms or phrases do you feel do not apply? (e.g., Do you pray for or with your friends? If so, in what circumstances? If not, why not?)

Consider having the youth break into pairs for this discussion, if you feel they'd be more comfortable sharing in a smaller group.

Have the youth tell about specific relationships that they can compare to Paul's relationships. Note that Paul's relationships were not necessarily between equals. For instance, Paul admitted that he could command Philemon to obey (verse 8). He also noted that Philemon owed Paul his very life (verse 19). Yet Paul claimed a relationship with Philemon that was based on love, especially the love of Christ. Ask: *Does your love for Christ, or your faith in Christ's love, have any impact upon your friendships?*

Exploring the Story (15–20 minutes)
OPTION A
Needed: newsprint and markers or chalkboard and chalk, Bibles, Bible study helps, paper, writing utensils
Survey the learners to discover what aspects of this letter they would like to know more about. List these on newsprint and assign a person or persons to each topic. These might include "Paul," "Philemon," "slavery in New Testament times," "imprisonment of Roman citizens," "Epaphras," etc.

Provide Bible dictionaries and other pertinent resources and invite the learners to read more about the subject in which they are interested. Also, make sure everyone has paper and a writing utensil. You may need to help the students use the resources, if they haven't used them before. Ask the youth to make some notes about what they discover, so that they can report back to the group. Invite them to consider in what ways their discoveries affect their ideas and understanding of Philemon.

Call them back together for a general discussion about their subject. Ask, *Has any of the information affected your interpretation of the letter to Philemon?*

OPTION B
Needed: Bibles
Some readers of Philemon will be disappointed that Paul did not comment on the evils of slavery. Instead, he sent Onesimus back to his master. (He does, however, indicate that their formerly unequal relationship could never be the same again.) Say, *What was Paul's motive for sending Onesimus back to Philemon? Did he do it because Roman law demanded it? Did he do it because Onesimus wanted to return but was afraid? We will never know. But one thing seems certain: Human institutions will be radically changed in Christ. Although Paul didn't tell how or why they should be changed, he believed they would be changed at the grassroots level— between human beings.*

Have the youth read Galatians 3:28 and Colossians 3:11. Compare these passages and the story of Onesimus to Luke 17:5-10. Ask: *What does Paul have to say about human institutions in these passages?* Compare slavery in human history to slavery in the kingdom of God, as Jesus seems to in the passage from Luke. Ask:
■ Can slavery be justified according to the master of the slaves?
■ Is the metaphor of "slave" any longer a helpful way to understand our role in the kingdom of God? If so, why? If not, what might be a better metaphor today, capturing the same concept with a different image?

Living the Story
(5–10 minutes)
OPTION A
Needed: information on mediation, conflict resolution, or peer mediation
Many high schools have instituted programs of peer mediation and peer counseling. In these programs, selected students are trained to mediate disputes between two students and even between students and school administration. Also, students are trained to counsel fellow students, mostly by practicing active listening skills.

Find out about such programs in your area, and encourage your students to get involved. If they are already involved, ask them to tell the others in your group about what they have learned and the experiences they have had. Plan some sessions during which you can teach the skills to your group and see how these skills affect their relationships. Be sure to close your session with prayer.

Some suggested resources: *Ready-to-Use Conflict Resolution Activities for Secondary Students* by Ruth Perlstein (Prentice-Hall Direct, 1996); *Peer Mediation Skills: Leader's Guide for Training Peer Mediators* by John De Marco (Hazelden Information and Educational Services, 1998); *Everything You Need to Know about Peer Mediation* by Nancy N. Rue (Rosen Grove, 1997). Try a search of the Internet using "peer mediation." Or check out the following sites: www.cruinstitute.org and www.coe.ufl.edu/CRPM/ CRPMhome.html.

OPTION B

Needed: "Guidelines for a Discussion about Our Basic Beliefs" handouts (optional)

Challenge your group to find a unity of purpose with a youth group from a very different church. If someone in your group knows someone from another church, perhaps she or he could help make a connection between the two groups. Otherwise, consult with your minister for help in contacting another church.

Spend this time deciding what you want to do and planning how to do it. You will then need to make arrangements and assignments for later. You might want to meet together and talk about basic beliefs, distributing copies of the "Guidelines for a Discussion about Our Basic Beliefs" handout or just sharing the information verbally. Send an invitation and arrange for refreshments. Be sure to have what you need for the discussion (markers, newsprint, statements of belief, etc.). Ask someone who is an excellent discussion leader to facilitate this meeting. To begin the meeting, you might ask a representative from each group to give a brief history of the Christian tradition as it has been lived out in their respective churches. Remind everyone that the main goal of the discussion is to dis-cover unity of purpose rather than to emphasize differences.

Or you may invite another youth group to join you in some sort of service project. Invite the other group to help with the project, eat together afterward, and debrief the experience. During the debriefing, ask how faith motivates service in the community.

Things to Ponder

This session will be more meaningful for youth who have struggled to articulate their faith and live by it as well as for those who have had to confront the issues of differences between different groups of Christians. Help youth to get in touch with these questions. Familiarize the youth with struggles, for instance, between Irish Catholics and Irish Protestants. Help them struggle with the contrast between hearing what Jesus said and doing what Jesus said.

Looking Ahead

Depending on which options you choose, you may have the class doing extensive work with clay. Be sure to get all the supplies necessary for these options in advance. Suggestions are made in the "You May Need" listing as well as in the related options themselves.

Listening Guide

Opening Address

1. Who is writing the letter?

2. What is his situation?

3. To whom is the letter addressed?

4. The writer asks for what two gifts from God for those receiving the letter?

Thanksgiving

5. The writer indicates that he engages in what spiritual practice?

6. For what, in particular, is the writer thankful?

7. What has the writer received because of those to whom he writes?

The Writer's Request

8. The writer appeals to his reader on the basis of _____ rather than command.

9. For whom does he appeal?

10. Cite at least two phrases that indicate the sort of relationship the writer has with the one for whom he is appealing.

11. The one for whom the writer pleads is a runaway _____ .

12. The writer wants the reader of this letter to receive the runaway back as a _____ .

13. If the runaway owes anything, who will repay it?

14. The writer indicates that the reader owes him even for his own self. What does that mean?

15. What does the writer expect the reader will do?

Closing

16. What does the writer hope to do one day soon?

17. Who else sends greetings besides the writer?

Guidelines for a Discussion about Our Basic Beliefs

The focus of this gathering is to learn about the basic beliefs of each church. Basic beliefs are the principles or symbols of faith that matter most in the daily life of congregational participants. Basic beliefs arise out of one's own experience of the holy.

Before you begin, make sure that you know everyone else's name. To help everyone relax and feel more comfortable with one another, be prepared to answer this question: *What is your most memorable church event?* The leader/facilitator will share his or her answer first, then proceed around the group and give everyone a chance to respond. (Of course, if someone does not want to say anything, that is okay.) If more than ten people are present, divide into smaller groups, being sure that smaller groups have an even mix from both of the churches/organizations involved.

The next step in the meeting will be to provide each individual with a copy of the Apostles' Creed and (if available) the creed or affirmation of faith of each church represented at the meeting. Each person will be given time to read these statements, and then you will be invited to circle the words and phrases that are most meaningful to you.

Your leader/facilitator will write the following examples of beliefs on newsprint and then lead a discussion on them.

Some basic beliefs might easily be expressed in keywords, like:

Creator	Savior	Holy Spirit	Holy Trinity
Sin	Grace	Redemption	Judgment

Others might express their basic beliefs with thematic keywords, like:

God is Love	Jesus	Friend	Growth
Forgiveness	Christian duty	Compassion	Prayer
Worship	Mission	Acceptance	Biblical inerrancy

Still other expressions of basic beliefs might be associated with images or symbols.

Cross	Dove	Empty tomb	Shepherd/Sheep

Finally, still other expressions of bedrock beliefs will be brief stories of life struggle and spiritual victory. These could include:

Experiences of healing	Release from addiction
Unexpected joy	Conviction of sin and awareness of forgiveness
Mystical unity	Rescue from disaster

Participants will be invited to call out words or phrases in each of these categories of belief as well as from the creedal statements that you have read. The leader/facilitator will write them on separate sheets of newsprint for each group, and then the larger group can compare the responses.

Ideas for this handout came from *Moving Off the Map: A Field Guide to Changing the Congregation* by Thomas G. Bandy (Nashville: Abingdon, 1998).

7. The Potter's Wheel

Bible Story: Jeremiah 18:1-6

Wallace Smith

A Story behind the Story

The story of Jeremiah visiting the potter's shop is perhaps the best-known passage from the Book of Jeremiah. The image of the clay being shaped by the gentle hands of the potter is a beautiful image for spiritual formation. And yet, in the image of the potter reshaping the vessel into something the potter is pleased with, we gloss over the part of the story where the potter destroys the original vessel. Suddenly, for that jarring moment, the hands are not so gentle! By reading only the upside of this story in Jeremiah, we lose sight of the prophecies of Jeremiah that seem dark and angry. Why should we pay attention to these more disquieting moments? After all, isn't that all past history?

Jeremiah, like most of the prophets, was mediating between a disobedient, even rebellious people and a God who was trying to work a purpose out in history. The Potter has jurisdiction over the clay (see Isaiah 45:9 and Romans 9:20-21), and if the clay is not shaping up correctly, the Potter will start over. Jeremiah's warning is clear: the recalcitrant people would be reshaped, and that reshaping is not always a comfortable process. It can even feel violent at times. Israel needed to be reshaped because injustice was widespread and God's people had alienated themselves from God (see Jeremiah 6:13-14; 11:1-13).

When you take in the wider context of Jerusalem in Jeremiah's time, and the words of the Lord to Jeremiah and the people of Israel throughout the book, the image of the potter and clay takes on new meaning. This is a story told during the destruction of an Israel that had turned away from God. The old had to be destroyed before the new vessel, pleasing to God, could take shape. But the new shape *would* be formed; God doesn't simply dispose of the clay. Through all the destruction and darkness in the Book of Jeremiah, there is a glimmer of hope that shines throughout. God would restore, reshape, and renew Israel if they would turn back to God. This is God's promise, God's covenant of salvation with God's people.

As Christians, we know that this covenant of restoration is continued through Jesus Christ and that we also need to remain open to God's constant reshaping in our lives. How do we participate in injustice, whether wittingly or unwittingly? Where do we need to be reshaped to be a part of God's purpose being worked out in history? What difference does our belief in Christ actually make to the living of these days?

- What is pleasing to God?
- Is God pleased with me?
- Am I happy with myself?
- Does God punish unfaithfulness? If so, how?
- What in myself do I want to change?
- What about my choices can lead to a better future?

YOU MAY NEED

- newspaper, waxed paper, or newsprint (for protecting table surface)
- waxed paper
- bowls of water and towels
- potter's wheel
- artist's clay (may be substituted with play dough if clay is not available)[1]
- CD player and CD of quiet Christian music of your choice (consider finding some that fits the themes of today's Scripture story)
- Bibles
- "Go Down to the Potter's House" handouts
- paper
- writing utensils
- "A Vessel That Is Pleasing" handouts
- newsprint and markers or chalkboard and chalk
- Bible study aids, such as commentaries, dictionaries, encyclopedias, etc.
- Bible concordance
- candle and matches
- ball of yarn or string
- copies of the lyrics for "Spirit of the Living God" or a similar hymn

Enter the Story

Take time before the session to read the story and to practice "praying the Scripture" in the process of *lectio divina* (Option A of "Telling the Story"). First take time to pray, breathe deeply, relax, and let all distractions melt away. Slowly read the Scripture (sometimes reading aloud to yourself helps) and let your mind and heart focus on any images or words that seem to come from the Scripture. Let that word or image be a focus for prayer, and reflect on your word or image throughout the day.

If you are using artist's clay during this session, take time to work the clay yourself before the session, so that you are comfortable with using the clay. Warm the clay with your hands, note the earthy feel of working with the clay, try forming different shapes, and use water to change the consistency of the clay if it gets too dry or sticky. Form a cup, bowl, vase, or other vessel as an example for the class and let it dry before the session. Take time to pray for your group, for each person in the group, and for their encounter with the Potter.

Setting the Stage (5–10 minutes)
OPTION A
Needed: tables, newspaper or newsprint, waxed paper, bowls of water, towels
As participants arrive, ask them to help set up your room as a "potter's shop." Save one area of the room to do Bible study and discussion in, but convert another into your art studio. Prepare tables by covering them with newspaper or newsprint,

and fill bowls with water. Have the waxed paper, towels, and water ready if you are using artist's clay.

Make sure each participant has a part in setting the room up for the activities that come later in the session. By having them participate, you are not only saving time for setup between activities later in the session but also the youth are literally "setting the stage" for the story encounter that will take place.

While you are setting up, ask if anyone has had experience with clay and sculpting before. Ask:
- What was it like?
- Was it easy or hard? Why?
- What was the hardest part?
- Did you have to destroy something midway through and start over? If so, how did that feel?

Ask the youth if they know what story in the Bible you may be focusing on today.

OPTION B
Needed: potter's wheel, clay, water, paper towels
A powerful way to experience the story of the potter and the clay is to have firsthand experience on a potter's wheel. Some art studios or arts and crafts supply stores may have portable wheels available for rent. You may have available to you a person in your church or community who is a potter or sculptor by profession or hobby and who could lend you a portable potter's wheel. Perhaps this person would even be willing to come to your session and teach simple and quick ways to work clay on a wheel. Begin the session with a demonstration of the potter's wheel, and then later, in Option B of "Reacting to the

Story" and "Connecting to the Story," participants may have a chance to work clay on the potter's wheel. Ask the youth if they've ever done so before, and invite them to describe their experiences. (If you have a guest artist, this person could also be "the potter" in Option B of "Telling the Story.")

Telling the Story (5–10 minutes)

OPTION A

Needed: Bibles

Invite the youth to read the Scripture in a process similar to *lectio divina,* which is a meditative approach to hearing and experiencing Scripture. Encourage the participants to find their own space in the area and get comfortable so that they will not be distracted by others. Give them these instructions: *Listen quietly, with your eyes closed, as I read today's story. I want you to concentrate on the Scripture as you hear it. It has a lot of visual images, so picture yourself in the story as it is happening.* Encourage the youth to relax and breathe deeply, perhaps even leading them through a series of relaxation and deep-breathing exercises before you begin. Open with a short time of silent prayer (or lead a prayer yourself) in order to focus their thoughts on the words of the story and ask God's help in hearing the message contained within. Then read the Jeremiah passage through slowly three times, with a pause between each reading. Then after the final reading and another pause, ask the participants to open their eyes and rejoin the large group, maintaining their quietness until the next instructions.

OPTION B

Needed: three volunteers, clay, "Go Down to the Potter's House" handouts

In this step, you'll be telling the story firsthand, using youth volunteers to act out the Scripture. The "Go Down to the Potter's House" handout is a direct adaptation of the Scripture from the New Revised Standard Version of the Bible, divided into a narrative. Make copies of the script for three participants.

Using volunteers from the class, you may need to ask the actors to arrive early for the session, so that they may get a head start on the short script. If that is not possible, simply select three volunteers from the class and give them a few moments to read and practice their part in a different space. When they are ready, invite them to tell the story to the larger group as Jeremiah, the potter, and the Lord.

Once they have finished their telling, have the class open their Bibles to the passage and read it through again themselves, to make sure they've gotten the full story.

Reacting to the Story (15–20 minutes)

OPTION A

Needed: Bibles, newsprint and markers or chalkboard and chalk

List on newsprint or chalkboard the words "potter," "potter's house," "clay," and "reworked clay." Invite the youth to add any other images from the passage they may think of, listing these images alongside the ones you just wrote. (This is the follow-up for Option A in "Telling the Story," but it can also work if you chose Option B.)

Once you've got several things listed (and the youth may not come up with any other than those you've already written), ask the youth to consider what these images might mean. Discuss each one in turn. For some images, the meaning might be quite clear; for other images, youth might have some disagreement or see nuances of difference. Remind the youth that this is okay, but use these differences to spur more in-depth discussion.

Invite a volunteer to read verses 1-4 again out loud. Ask the participants: *How does God speak to Jeremiah through the work of the potter?* Discuss any questions the youth may have about the first four verses of Scripture. Then read the Scripture again, this time adding verses 5 and 6. What is their first reaction to the images of the Scripture as a whole? What do they think the message of the Scripture is?

OPTION B
(If you choose this, choose Option B in "Connecting to the Story.")
Needed: clay, newspaper or waxed paper, water, towels
Give each participant a lump of clay. Invite them to create something out of the clay, encouraging them to create anything they want, perhaps creating an image from the Scripture. Before they complete their masterpieces, stop the group and have each person roll his or her creation back into a lump of clay. Ask the youth how it felt to create something and then destroy the creation. Take time to listen and react to what each person shares.

Encourage all responses, whether their impressions are negative ("I didn't want to mess up my sculpture") or positive ("I'm glad I could start over and do better"). Now, ask the youth what opportunities or possibilities they see in the lump of clay before them. Finally, ask the youth what they think the point of the Scripture was and what God was teaching Jeremiah. Remember, there may be differences of opinion here, and that's okay!

Connecting to the Story (15–20 minutes)
OPTION A
Needed: writing utensils, paper, "A Vessel That Is Pleasing" handouts, CD player and CD (optional)
We have an "earthy" connection with the image of the pottery being formed on a potter's wheel—we may consider ourselves as the vessel being formed. Invite the youth to take a copy of the "Vessel That Is Pleasing" handout and a writing utensil and find a private place within your class space to do their work. Remind them that they will need to be quiet and respect each other's privacy. Explain to the youth that they will be filling out this handout primarily for themselves, but they will have the opportunity to share their responses if they so choose. You might consider playing some suitable background music while they do their reflecting, especially if you can find Christian music that reflects some of the themes of the story.

After the youth have had several minutes to fill out their handouts, bring them back together into a larger group (or pairs or triads) to share their responses. Remember, sharing is not mandatory. Some youth may feel their answers are too personal to share in public. If this is the case, invite them to share a hypothetical situation. Ask, *How might someone need to be shaped by God?*

OPTION B
(This option follows Option B in "Reacting to the Story.")
Needed: clay (or play dough), newspaper or waxed paper, water, towels, CD player and CD (optional)
Now that the youth have gone through the process of creating and destroying their sculpture with the clay, give them the opportunity to start over. This is their second chance with the clay, and they can make a new creation that is a symbol of their connection to the story. We have two perspectives in the story to connect with: (1) the connection with the potter (verses 3-4), as we make choices to start over; and (2) the connection with Jeremiah (verses 5-6), who learns that God is at work in creation and salvation, able to "reshape" Israel. How do we connect with opportunities in our own lives to start over? You may want to play some quiet background music on CD as described in Option A.

After the creations are finished, offer an opportunity for the youth to share their creations with the larger group, if they so choose. Be sure to have the youth refrain from making negative comments on their classmates' creations.

Exploring the Story
(15–20 minutes)
OPTION A
Needed: Bibles, Bible study aids, newsprint and markers or chalkboard and chalk
The larger story found in the Book of Jeremiah and the message of Jeremiah himself may be difficult to understand in one session, yet it is important to explore what was going on in the world of Jeremiah. What was happening in Israel in Jeremiah's time? What was Jeremiah's message or prophecy?

Take this time to explore other stories and events in the Book of Jeremiah, perhaps including the following: Jeremiah 1:1-10; 6:1-15; 8:18–9:2; 18; and 30–31. You may need to parcel out the Scriptures among members of the group and then have participants share their findings. You may also want to use Bible commentaries or other study aids that are available to you.

After the group has done some background research, create a "map" of the historical background to Jeremiah on newsprint or a chalkboard. Ask the youth, *What kinds of injustices might be occurring that are displeasing to God?* When they have a fairly good background, have them consider this: *How does this passage reflect a hope for justice or liberation?*

OPTION B
Needed: Bibles, Bible concordances, paper, writing utensils, newsprint and markers or chalkboard and chalk
In groups of two or three, explore other stories of creation and

salvation that use images of pottery, clay, dust, earth, etc. Have the groups brainstorm a list of possible word images to look up, writing these on newsprint or a chalkboard. Make available concordances for the youth to use in order to find Scriptures that they can relate to the story of potter and clay. Encourage each group to come up with at least three other places in the Bible where these "earthy" images are used to describe God's response to injustice, God's creating and saving power, or God's liberation. (If the groups have trouble finding Scriptures, or if you do not have a concordance available, here are some Scriptures to look up: Genesis 2:7; Psalm 103:14; Ecclesiastes 3:20; Isaiah 45:9; 64:8; John 9:6; Romans 9:21; 1 Corinthians 15:47; 2 Corinthians 4:7,16; 5:17.) Compare and contrast the passages with Jeremiah 18:1-6. What are the similarities and differences?

Finally, have the small groups brainstorm modern imagery that could say the same thing. As if they were Jeremiah, what might God show them in today's world to express the same concept? Rather than a potter's house, they might be taken where?

**Living the Story
(5–10 minutes)**
OPTION A
Needed: candle, matches, ball of string, copies of lyrics for "Spirit of the Living God" or similar hymn
Gather the youth into a circle, with a candle on the table or in the center of the floor. Invite the youth to silence as you light the candle and

briefly review some of the activities you've done during the session. Ask the youth to reflect on the "threads" or connections of justice and liberation in the story. Pass the ball of string around the group, explaining that each person who receives the ball should offer a one-word or short-phrase response to the connections of creation and change in the story. When they pass the ball on, they are to maintain hold on part of the string. When the string connects the whole circle, read again the Scripture (Jeremiah 18:1-6) and sing as a prayer "Spirit of the Living God" or a similar hymn, or pray using the words of the song.

OPTION B
(This activity follows Option B in "Reacting to the Story" and "Connecting to the Story.")
Needed: clay sculptures, table, paper, writing utensils
Share the clay creations in this time of affirmation. Set up a sculpture gallery on a table with a blank piece of paper next to each creation. Give each youth a writing utensil, and ask them to be seated as you take a few moments to review the activities and highlights of this session. Invite the youth to go around the table and pause at each sculpture to write a few words of affirmation for each artist's work. After they've done so, have them move back into a circle, standing with the sculptures in the center of the circle. Read Jeremiah 18:1-6 again, or ask a volunteer to do so, as you invite the rest of the youth to reflect upon the sculptures in front of them while they hear the words of the

story one more time. Close the session with a prayer of thanks for the ways our liberating God can reshape and renew us.

Things to Ponder

The Book of Jeremiah, and the image of God as angry and destructive, can be pretty rough without the hope of salvation that comes in the image of reshaping or recreating the clay in the Potter's hands. This session may also open discussion along the lines of second chances. Another issue to be sensitive to is the connection between the image of the Potter shaping our inner and outer selves with the issues of each participant's own self-image, either positive or negative.

Looking Ahead

Depending on which options you choose, there may be some items to prepare ahead of class (such as chopping up pieces of fruit or preparing supplies for a step). Please be sure to make your session plan in as far advance as possible to give you adequate time for preparation.

Note

1. A good type of artist's clay to use is Air Dry Modeling Clay, which you can find at your local art or education supply store. One brand is AMACO, standing for American Art and Clay Company. At the time of this writing, twenty-five pounds of clay sells for $10 or under. When estimating quantity, be mindful that ten pounds is sufficient for thirty people.

~~~~~~

Go Down to the Potter's House

Needed: three volunteers, clay (or play dough), potter's wheel (optional)

Cast

The potter, Jeremiah, and the Lord.

Setting

A potter's shop. The potter sits on a chair or on the floor and quietly
works and shapes a lump of clay while Jeremiah tells the story.

Jeremiah:	The Lord told me . . .
Lord (to Jeremiah):	Go to the pottery shop, and when you get there, I will tell you what to say to the people.
Jeremiah:	I went there and saw the potter making clay pots on his wheel. *[He watches the potter making a pot or bowl, then clump and rework the clay to start over or make something else.]* And whenever the clay would not take the shape he wanted, he would change his mind and form it into some other shape. *[He pauses again, watching the potter.]* Then the Lord told me to say . . .
Lord and Jeremiah in unison:	People of Israel, I, the Lord, have power over you just as a potter has power over clay. *[They point toward potter.]*

A Vessel That Is Pleasing

How God is shaping my life . . .

Places in my life I would like to reshape . . .

How I can be a vessel that is pleasing to God . . .

8. Sermon on the Mount

Bible Story: Matthew 4:23–5:16

Denise Janssen

A Story behind the Story

The idea of blessing is among the oldest concepts in the Hebrew Scriptures. We find it woven into many of the familiar stories—Cain and Abel, Noah, Abraham and Sarah, Isaac and his sons, and on and on. It crops up again in the New Testament when the Zebedee brothers, urged on by their mother, ask Jesus to bless their faithfulness with places of honor in his kingdom. People have wrestled for centuries with making sense of the good times and the struggles in their lives. We still find ourselves wrestling today.

Coming off a forty-day temptation in the desert, Jesus called some disciples and began a whirlwind tour of the hot spots of Galilee. As he taught and healed, people from farther away began to hear about him and bring their sick friends, looking for Jesus to bless them by healing them of their affliction. It is in this context that Jesus preached the Sermon on the Mount.

In his teaching in Matthew 5–7, Jesus spent time laying out for his hearers what it really means to be blessed—and how bearers of the blessing can be recognized. His disciples and the others gathered there must have been baffled as Jesus created the list of those who should be considered blessed, specifically in 5:1-16. Absent from the list were the usual suspects—those with possessions and authority, those with lots of children (especially sons), and those people who seemed to have good luck. Instead, the list was full of the last, the lost, and the least of society—mourners and meek folks, wimpy peacemakers and merciful people, the persecuted and those who struggled to understand what is right instead of jumping on the Pharisees bandwagon.

Jesus himself was beginning a journey with this sermon that was going to take some twists and turns that wouldn't make him look very blessed. Yet, in the end, the blessing of salvation extends even to us through God's actions in the person of Jesus.

Enter the Story

Read the text through once (either the entire Sermon on the Mount or only the Beatitudes), then go back through it, noting any words that seem unusual or worth additional research into their meanings. Read the text through again from another translation or paraphrase, looking again at ways the words are used to create an image. Now read the text one more time, looking for words that evoke emotion for you. Write these down and reflect on why these words strike you more profoundly. (An example might be the word "mourn" if you've recently experienced the loss of a loved one.) Spend a moment praying for the youth and their lives.

Sit for a moment in darkness until your eyes have adjusted. Then turn on a light. Write in your journal about the effect of the light on the darkness. Consider ways the imagery of light is used in Scripture, and think about which of these is particularly meaningful for you. Consider those people who have been light in your life. Thank God for them and for bringing true light into the world.

Setting the Stage (5–10 minutes)
OPTION A
Needed: newsprint and markers
Write the words *bless, blessed,* and *blessings* at the top of a sheet of newsprint. (Use multiple sheets and divide your class into smaller discussion groups if your class is larger than eight people.) Lay the newsprint on a table or on the floor with the markers on top of it. Encourage youth to brainstorm the different ways these words are used in our culture today, writing or drawing each idea on the newsprint. You may help them get started with an example, such as saying "Bless you" when someone sneezes. As youth begin to run out of ideas, have them turn the newsprint over and attempt to come up with a definition for these words that encompasses the variety of meanings they discovered.

OPTION B
Needed: salt, sugar, and lemon juice, each in a separate small bowl; fruit of various kinds cut into small pieces; paper and writing utensils
Ask youth to taste a little of the salt. Then ask them to write a description of the flavor of salt without using any form of the word *salt.* When everyone is finished, have the youth share their definitions with one another. Together the group may choose the description

that most accurately describes the flavor of salt.

Share with the group that the word *salary* comes from the ration of salt that a Roman soldier was given as part of his compensation. Salt was so important and so valuable that it was actually considered a fringe benefit (like health insurance today) to which Roman soldiers were entitled.

Then set out the dishes with sugar and lemon. Ask youth to write descriptions of the flavors of each without using any form of the words *sugar* or *lemon.* Was it easier or more difficult to describe the flavors of sugar and lemon in this manner than it was to describe the flavor of salt?

Follow the same process with the fruit, and ask the youth to compare the difficulty of the task with those just done.

Ask: *When Jesus told his listeners they were the salt of the earth, what was he saying about them?*

Telling the Story (5–10 minutes)
OPTION A
Needed: "Antiphonal Beatitudes" handouts, writing utensils
Form two groups and have those groups face each other. Hand out copies of "Antiphonal Beatitudes." Designate the groups as Group 1 and Group 2; you will read the "Leader" sections.

Remind the youth that church sanctuaries centuries ago were often constructed so the congregation sat facing each other on either side of the aisle. As the youth read the handout, encourage them to listen carefully to the words of this

POSSIBLE YOUTH CONTACT POINTS
- Does God think I'm special (blessed)?
- What value is there to the difficult things in my life?
- Does God care that I'm experiencing difficulty?
- Where is God when I'm struggling?
- What impact do my actions have on others?
- How will I make all the complex choices I need to make in the next few years?

YOU MAY NEED
- newsprint and markers
- paper
- writing utensils
- Bibles
- Bible study tools (NRSV concordance, one-volume commentary, one-volume Bible dictionary)
- several Bible versions, including contemporary language translations
- small bowls of salt, lemon, and sugar
- cut-up pieces of fruit, representing a variety of flavors
- small pieces of paper prepared with stick figures and descriptions (see Option B, "Reacting to the Story")
- Antiphonal Beatitudes" handouts
- "With Lenten Ears" handouts
- construction paper
- scissors
- markers
- glue
- candles and matches

story, underlining any that jump out to them as they read. Youth should keep the handouts if you plan to use Option A under "Exploring the Story."

OPTION B

Needed: paper, writing utensils, Bibles

Explain to the youth that the Beatitudes are a section of Scripture that's thick with "loaded" words—words that mean more than just what they appear to say. The word *blessed* is an example of a loaded word; no one in Jesus' day would have said that one who mourned was blessed. Jesus was using a word to mean something new, helping his hearers to understand something new about what it means to be blessed. In Jesus' day, a person might know that he or she was blessed if that person had a lot of money or possessions. Sometimes today we say that folks with lots of material possessions are "blessed," too. But to say that one who was poor in some way was blessed, or to say that one who mourned was blessed, represented a new way of thinking that redefined people's notion of God's blessing.

As you read the story or have youth read it, ask them to jot down other loaded phrases they hear as the text is read. Alternatively, you may want to make a photocopy of the text (from the New Revised Standard Version) for each youth and ask them to circle the loaded phrases in the text. Keep the handouts if you plan to use Option B under "Exploring the Story."

Reacting to the Story (15–20 minutes)

OPTION A

Needed: "With Lenten Ears" handouts, writing utensils

When Jesus preached the text we call the Sermon on the Mount, the disciples hadn't been disciples for very long (Matthew 4:18-22). Hearing his words now, they were probably moved by them. Someone even remembered them to record them for us. However, after following Jesus for several years, they likely heard these words differently based on their experiences of and with Jesus.

The purpose of this handout is to get youth thinking about the text from the perspective of the disciples during Jesus' last days. The disciples likely recalled snippets from Jesus' sermon during these turbulent days and heard them in new ways as a result of their various experiences. The youth may or may not know much about the events of Jesus' last week. If you are doing this session during Lent, they will be hearing the stories about that crucial week; otherwise, you may want to direct their attention to Matthew 26–28. Encourage youth to respond honestly on their handouts, but don't push them to share if they aren't ready to do so. You will want to keep this handout to use with Option A of "Exploring the Story."

OPTION B

Needed: Bibles, descriptive papers, paper, writing utensils

Prior to class, create small pieces of paper with stick figures on one side and one of the following descriptions on the back side. (The paper should be thick enough so that the description on one side doesn't show through to the stick figure on the other side.)

1. Mercenary Roman soldier
2. Young widow whose husband was killed in a tragic accident
3. Elderly woman
4. Boy celebrating his bar mitzvah
5. Slave (works without pay)
6. Wealthy landowner
7. Scholar and teacher
8. Maidservant

Give each participant one of the prepared pieces of paper, asking students to share if you have more than eight in the class. Ask each person to reread the Scripture, trying to hear what the person described on his or her paper would hear. Discuss the following:

■ Which beatitude would be especially meaningful to your character?
■ Which beatitude would trouble him or her?
■ Which one would the character question most?

Connecting with the Story (15–20 minutes)

OPTION A
Needed: newsprint for each person, markers, Bibles

Ask youth to choose a disciple or other person who spent time with Jesus and with whom they especially connect. For example, one girl may say she relates more closely with Peter because she is overly confident of her ability to follow Jesus but turns her back on her faith when things get too hot. You may need to offer some Scripture passages from Matthew for youth to refer to in finding particular characters.

Ask the youth to draw a stick figure on the page of newsprint to represent themselves. Using arrows to point to parts of their stick figure's body (remind them to use good taste), have them describe aspects of their connection with the biblical characters in light of the Beatitudes you've just read and their character's actions in the Gospel story. For example, the girl mentioned above might draw an arrow to the heart and label it with the words *weak heart*. Invite youth to share their drawings, if they wish.

OPTION B
Needed: construction paper, scissors, markers, glue

The Beatitudes have been loved, and often even memorized, by generations of Christians. Each one can have a depth of meaning that comes only from having been lived with throughout one's years. The way a youth might look at this passage might be very different from the way a septuagenarian might interpret it.

Offer the youth art supplies and invite them to each choose one part of the passage (4:23–5:16) that they find the most meaningful to them. It should be only one verse or even just a part of a verse. For example, one who had just lost a grandparent might choose 5:4, whereas someone who is feeling the need for more self-confidence might choose 5:13a (using only the phrase "you are the salt of the earth").

Once they have chosen their verse, invite them to write it on the piece of construction paper and decorate it in some meaningful way. Encourage them to attempt to memorize their chosen verse as well so that they might remember it during troubled times throughout their lives. Once they've finished their creations, invite them to share why they chose the verse they did (if they want to share) and tell what meaning their decorations have.

Exploring the Story (15–20 minutes)

OPTION A
(Choose this option if you did Option A in "Telling the Story" and "Reacting to the Story" above.)
Needed: handouts from previous steps, writing utensils, Bible reference tools
Referring to the handouts the youth marked up in "Telling the Story" and "Reacting to the Story" (both Option A), ask youth to share with each other the words that jumped out at them, loaded phrases, or "Scripture-speak" they found.

Invite them to think about where else in Scripture they have heard each phrase or word. For example, someone may mention the phrase "kingdom of heaven" and remember that Jesus told several parables about it later on.

Using the Bible reference tools and working in small groups, help the youth search for the phrases they picked out. A concordance, for example, will help the youth find other uses of the same phrase in the Bible. Looking first at other places these phrases are used in Matthew, and then other places in the Gospels and the rest of the New Testament, encourage youth to explore the possible meanings of each Beatitude.

Youth may not have time to finish this during the session—the idea is to spark their curiosity and get them thinking about the Beatitudes in a new way.

OPTION B
(Choose this option if you used Option B in "Telling the Story.")
Needed: marked-up photocopies of the Scripture text from Option B above, several other translations or paraphrases of this Scripture, newsprint and markers
Ask youth to select a Bible translation or paraphrase they would like to use and then read the text again from it quietly to themselves. (Be sure that you have some modern language versions, such as *The Message* or *The Cotton Patch Gospel*.) Youth may select several different versions to read, trading and sharing resources. First, have someone read each verse from the NRSV. Then ask participants with other versions to read theirs aloud (only that particular verse), noting on the newsprint interesting ways another version illuminates a particular concept through its wording. Pay particular attention to the marked words from the handouts. Do this for all the verses, hearing the text from as many different translations and paraphrases as possible. Then use another sheet of newsprint and invite the youth to rewrite the Beatitudes in their own words, using contemporary imagery where appropriate. You might want to share the product of this with the congregation in worship, if possible.

Living the Story (5–10 minutes)

OPTION A
Needed: candles for each participant (candles used for candlelight

services in many churches are best), matches or lighter, Bible
Have participants stand in a circle and give each (including yourself) an unlit candle. Using the matches, light the candle of the person to your right. Read Matthew 5:3, including the name of that person in the verse. For example, "Blessed are the poor in spirit, Jenny, for theirs is the kingdom of heaven." Pass the Bible to your left, then light your candle from the lit candle of the person on your right as the person on your left reads the next verse with your name inserted. Go around the circle, reading each Beatitude separately (repeating some, if you need to, in order for each person's name to be used and each person's candle to be lit).

Note: For safety reasons, make sure a candle is always lit *after* the one holding it has read. You don't want a youth trying to hold the Bible, read, and hold a lit candle all at the same time!

Use verses 13-16 as a single reading. Close with a prayer and dismiss the group by saying, *You are the light of the world—go from here and let your light shine.* Ask the youth to blow out their candles one at a time until all are extinguished.

OPTION B

Needed: salt

Note: Depending on your congregation's policies and protocols, you may want to think carefully about where you do this activity. Consider doing it outdoors or in a place that is easily swept.

Give each youth a small amount of salt in the palm of one hand.

Once everyone has salt, invite them to mingle around the group and sprinkle a pinch of salt gently on the shoulder of each person they meet. As they do this, they should offer this blessing to the person: *You are the salt of the earth.* Continue mingling until most people have salted one another, and then close by forming a circle for prayer. As you prepare to pray, encourage youth to keep their eyes open and look around at one another, thinking about times when each person in the group may have been salt and light for them. Close with a prayer time using the theme of salt and light.

Things to Ponder

Youth struggle constantly with issues of self-acceptance. Even seemingly confident youth crave words of blessing from other youth and adults, particularly those they respect. Consider finding a way this week to offer each youth a blessing—words that tell them that they are special and their lives mean something. Perhaps that might be a simple note to each youth. Or maybe you could make a point of calling each youth on the phone over the next couple of weeks just to hear about their lives and affirm them in the little things they celebrate.

Looking Ahead

Depending on which options you choose, you may need to find recordings of several contemporary Christian songs. The suggestions and ideas as to how to locate them are all listed in the "You May Need" section of the next session.

Antiphonal Beatitudes

Leader: When Jesus saw the crowds, he went up the mountain, and after he sat down, his disciples came to him. Then he began to speak, and taught them, saying:

Group 1: Blessed are the poor in spirit,

Group 2: for theirs is the kingdom of heaven.

Group 1: Blessed are those who mourn,

Group 2: for they will be comforted.

Group 1: Blessed are those who hunger and thirst for righteousness,

Group 2: for they will be filled.

Group 1: Blessed are the merciful,

Group 2: for they will receive mercy.

Group 1: Blessed are the pure in heart,

Group 2: for they will see God.

Group 1: Blessed are the peacemakers,

Group 2: for they will be called the children of God.

Group 1: Blessed are those who are persecuted for righteousness' sake,

Group 2: for theirs is the kingdom of heaven.

Group 1: Blessed are you when people revile you and persecute you and utter all kinds of evil against you falsely on my account.

Group 2: Rejoice and be glad, for your reward is great in heaven, for in the same way they persecuted the prophets who were before you.

All: You are the salt of the earth;

Group 1: but if salt has lost its taste, how can its saltiness be restored? It is no longer good for anything, but is thrown out and trampled under foot.

All: You are the light of the world.

Group 2: A city built on a hill cannot be hid. No one after lighting a lamp puts it under a bushel basket, but on the lampstand, and it gives light to all in the house.

Leader: In the same way, let your light shine before others, so that they may see your good works and give glory to your Father in heaven.

~~~~

With Lenten Ears

The Beatitudes take on special meanings and nuances when understood through the lens of Jesus' last days. Regardless of what time of year we are in, every story we hear of Jesus is colored by our knowledge of his crucifixion. Before looking at these questions, turn this page over and write down all the questions that come to your mind after hearing the text read today. Remember that any question is okay and God welcomes our questions (they are more like signs of faith than indications of a lack of faith).

Next, ponder the following questions as you reread the text with Lenten ears.

1. What does Jesus mean by "poor in spirit"? During the larger Lenten story, when are the disciples "poor in spirit"?

2. When are the disciples in mourning during the larger story of Jesus' death and resurrection?

3. When are the disciples hungry and thirsty for righteousness during the larger Lenten story?

4. When are the disciples merciful? When are they peacemakers? When are they persecuted for righteousness' sake? When are they reviled or persecuted on account of their connection with Jesus?

5. When all these things happen to them, what do you suppose they hear in the Beatitudes? What would you hear if you were mourning, for example?

6. In light of what happened in the disciples' lives during the Lenten story, do you think Jesus' pronouncement of them as salt of the earth and light of the world was prescriptive (encouraging them to be like that) or descriptive (using these euphemisms to tell them how he perceived them)? What difference would it make?

9. Doers, Not Just Hearers
Bible Story: James 1:22–2:26

Mark Luera

A Story behind the Story

It is hard to imagine what Christianity was like in its earliest years—after the resurrection of Jesus but before any of the New Testament was written. The Letter of James may come closest to giving us a window on that ancient time.

True, many Bible scholars disagree about the author's identity or the exact circumstances of the writing. They ask, "Did James, the brother of the Lord, write the letter? Do we have any evidence that the letter was in circulation before the first generation of Christians passed away?"

Whatever their conclusions, however, James's witness has had an impact upon every generation of Christians. Its moral conviction and its clear understanding of God as the Creator of the world, and as the center of every righteous human endeavor, still stands. To read James is to experience the joy of knowing that a real relationship with God is possible within a supportive and nurturing community of believers. In fact, James offers the reader a clear choice between "the world" and "God."

Since Jesus was raised from the dead, living for God means living by the words of Jesus, especially his commandment to love your neighbor as yourself, which James refers to as the "royal law" (2:8). It is not enough, James says, to know the words of Jesus and admire them. We must do what Jesus says in order to be a "friend of God" as Abraham was (2:21-23).

James insists that living for God should take place within a community of believers that continually seeks to save and include the poor, the orphaned, and the widowed. Thus James stands in the great tradition of the prophets, who believed that the law was given by God to preserve the lives of the poor and oppressed and make us aware of our fundamental relationships to God and one another.

God has provided all the guidance we need to live in right relationship with God and others. Most especially, God has done so in the words of Jesus. If we say that we are followers of Jesus, we will, at all costs, do what Jesus said. James makes it sound so simple . . . and perhaps it is!

Enter the Story

The Letter of James tolerates no distinction between faith and action. Allegiance to Christ means obedience to Christ—an obedience that is readily observable by all.

James has a clear notion of what God demands of us: "care for orphans and widows in their distress" (1:27). It rather vehemently claims that one's religion is worthless if one does not act according to the "royal law" of loving your neighbor (2:8).

As you read James 1:22–2:26, note your emotional response to the author's forceful proclamation. Do you find yourself agreeing with him or wanting to argue another approach to the life of faith?

Liberation of our spirits comes when self-centered religion becomes other-centered religion. Concern for others inevitably involves us in issues of justice. Orphans and widows suffer distress not just because of personal grief but also because they are excluded from access to the resources needed for survival. Keep all of these things in mind as you read the passage for yourself.

Setting the Stage (5–10 minutes)
OPTION A
Perhaps you have heard the old parental saying "Do as I say, not as I do." James seems to want to make the alternative point: "Do as *you* say."

To help prepare the learners for their discussion of James, play a Follow the Leader sort of game. The leader will tell the group to do one thing while he or she demonstrates something else. The followers are to do what the leader *says,* not what he or she *does.* This is more difficult than it sounds!

For instance, as the leader says, "Clap your hands," over and over, she might snap her fingers. The followers are to try to disregard what they are seeing and instead do what the leader is saying. The leader might say, "Scratch your chin," while scratching his head. The leader might say, "Touch your nose," while pulling her ear.

You may wish to act as leader yourself to begin the game and then invite other members of the group to give it a try. Whoever is the leader should be prepared to

move quickly from one motion to the next and not get mixed up himself or herself!

The point of the exercise is to demonstrate that children are most likely to do what their parents (and other adults) do, not what they say.

OPTION B
Needed: skin stain
Try either or both of these exercises to set the stage for your study of James:

1. Stain each person as he or she enters the room. Use henna or a permanent marker to draw a Christian symbol (such as a fish, a cross, or three interlocking circles) on the back of each person's right hand. Tell them the stain will remind them of their faith. Engage the group in a discussion of the meaning of the symbol you have chosen. Contrast this stain with the stain mentioned in James 1:27.

2. Ask class members to choose partners. Have the two face each other and shake hands. Immediately after shaking hands, they should stand back to back. Now have them describe their partner's hair color, eye color, outfit, demeanor, etc. James points out in 1:23 that we often are like those who look at themselves in a mirror but, as soon as they quit looking, forget what they looked like! So we forget what it is we are to do for Christ.

Telling the Story (5–10 minutes)
OPTION A
Needed: Bibles, paper, writing utensils
Ahead of class time, find a volunteer who will prepare to read the

POSSIBLE YOUTH CONTACT POINTS
- How would I sum up my faith?
- In what ways can I put my faith into action?
- What contrasts are there between the life of faith and the way of the world?
- Is religion more a matter of acts of charity or acts of devotion?

YOU MAY NEED
- Bibles
- skin stain (such as henna or permanent marker)
- a volunteer prepared to read James 1:22–2:26
- newsprint or chalkboard
- markers or chalk
- blank writing paper
- writing utensils
- *The New Testament Message* by Eugene Peterson
- assorted props for skits (optional)
- video camera and editing capabilities (optional)
- "A Study of James" handouts
- "Heroes Depicted in Movies and Books" handouts
- poster boards (one white, one red)
- sticky note pads
- computer with access to the Internet (optional)
- CDs of Christian songs such as "I Could Sing of Your Love Forever" by Delirious?, "Hands and Feet" by Audio Adrenaline, and "El Salvador" by Phil Joel[1]
- CD of "The Houseplant Song" by Audio Adrenaline or another song with the theme of being a neighbor[2]
- CD player
- lyrics of chosen Christian songs (optional)
- Bible commentary on James
- candles and matches (or lighter)
- bowls of warm water
- soft washcloths

passage from James 1:22–2:26. This volunteer will want to become quite familiar with the passage so that he or she can give it appropriate expression and tone.

Before the reader begins, distribute paper and pencils or pens to the learners and request that they take notes while the reader reads. Each should divide the paper into two columns. At the top of one column, they should write "How Christians Should Act." At the top of the second column, they should write "How Christians Act Hypocritically." Then they should write words and phrases in the appropriate column as the text is read.

For instance, as one student hears 1:22 read, he might jot down "be doers" in column 1. In column 2, he might write "not just hearers." As a youth hears verse 1:26, she might write in column 2 "unbridled tongues." As another hears 2:8, he might write in column 1 "fulfill the royal law."

At this point in the session, ask the volunteer to do his or her reading. This person should pause at logical stopping places to give the listeners time to make notes. Let participants stop the reader and ask him or her to repeat a verse if they would like.

OPTION B
Needed: Bibles, paper, writing utensils, newsprint and markers or chalkboard and chalk (optional)
Make sure everyone has a Bible or a copy of James 1:22–2:26. Also, distribute paper and pencils or pens. Tell the learners that you want them to read the passage, or parts of it, three times. First, read through the

entire passage. Write down three words or phrases that sum up your first impression of James.

As you read through the passage the second time, try to find natural divisions. Think in terms of scenes that could be dramatized. Choose a section of the passage that you think might be interesting to dramatize. A section could be anything from a phrase to several verses. You might want to illustrate 1:22, for instance, by writing verbs on a chalkboard while someone does that action and someone else merely listens. Or you might act out verses 2:2-4 by having someone portray a wealthy person coming into an assembly and being well treated, followed by someone portraying a poor person who is shabbily treated.

Read that section a third time and write down ideas for acting it out or illustrating the idea with a drama, sketch, pantomime, etc.

Reacting to the Story (15–20 minutes)
OPTION A
(This option best follows Option A of "Telling the Story.")
Needed: paper, writing utensils, a copy of The New Testament Message *(optional)*
If you chose Option A in "Telling the Story," use your notes to paraphrase the passage. A paraphrase restates the meaning of the passage without using the same words or images or metaphors. A paraphrase often puts the passage in words and images that might be more readily understandable to a contemporary audience.

Participants will need writing paper and pens or pencils. Since the passage is quite long, you might allow participants to choose a section to paraphrase. If you do so, be sure the entire passage gets covered. To give the youth an idea of what a good paraphrase looks like, obtain a copy of *The New Testament Message with Psalms and Proverbs* by Eugene Peterson (NavPress, 1998) for them to read.

OPTION B
(This option best follows Option B of "Telling the Story.")
Needed: Bibles, props for skits (optional), video camera and editing capabilities (optional)
If you chose Option B of "Telling the Story," choose directors for each scene. Let the directors choose one or more actors (these could include the director as well). The director might simply sketch the scene for the actors and let them improvise, or the director might read the passage from the Bible while the actors pantomime specific actions. Let the director use his or her imagination to portray the gist of the passage he or she has chosen. Provide rudimentary costuming, if possible—robes, jewelry, ragged clothing, etc.

Of course, you can divide the passage up in many different ways. If it seems easier or more effective to make assignments, the sections might divide as follows: 1:22-25; 1:26-27; 2:1-7; 2:8-13; 2:14-17; 2:18-26. If the directors leave out some part of the passage that someone thinks is important, let her or him be a director and dramatize that part of the passage.

You might want to develop one or all of these presentations into chancel dramas to be used in worship or at a church fellowship dinner. Or consider filming these vignettes and editing them into presentations for worship. You would need video equipment and perhaps video editing capabilities as well as a video projector.

Connecting to the Story (15–20 minutes)
OPTION A
(If choosing this option, you will want to choose Option A of "Living the Story.")
Needed: newsprint and markers or chalkboard and chalk, white and red poster board, pads of sticky notes
Write verse 27 of chapter 1 on newsprint or on a chalkboard. Read it aloud to the class.

Label two sheets of newsprint, each with one of the two words *orphans* and *widows*. Divide the class into two smaller groups, each with one of the newsprints, and invite them to decide who might be included in their category today. They should write their answers on the newsprint. For instance, "orphans" might include abused children, while "widows" might include the elderly who cannot take care of themselves. Invite the youth to tell some ways in which they have personally cared for "orphans and widows." Have the subgroups share their results with the class as a whole.

Hang a white poster board and a red poster board on opposite sides of the room. Give each participant a pad of sticky notes. Invite the youth to write on the note sheets some ways in which they feel "stained" by the world. These might fall into two broad categories: temptations (for example, movies, rock songs, advertisements, drugs, violence) and mistreatment (teasing, exclusion by the popular kids, unfair treatment by coaches and teachers). They should post these on the red poster board.

Next, invite the youth to write down ways in which we can prevent or protect ourselves from being "stained" by the world. These could include Bible study, worship, prayer, carefully choosing movies, etc. Post these on the white poster board. When everyone has had a chance to post something on both boards, read the notes aloud and talk about these comments and ideas.

OPTION B
Needed: CDs as listed below, CD player, lyric sheets (if possible), computer with Internet connection (optional)
Canvass the participants in the group to see what they know about Christian rock bands and their lyrics. Compare the lyrics to "I Could Sing of Your Love Forever" by Delirious? to the lyrics of "Hands and Feet" by Audio Adrenaline. Talk about the similarities and differences. (Having the lyrics written out in advance will help in these discussions.)

If you are able to in the classroom, visit the websites of various Christian rock bands (such as the Newsboys at www.newsboys.com). Note, specifically, Phil Joel's trip to El Salvador, and play the song of that name from his CD *Watching Over You*. Investigate ways in which band members live out their faith.

Exploring the Story (15–20 minutes)
OPTION A
Needed: Bible commentaries, "A Study of James" handouts, Bibles, paper, writing utensils
Provide an opportunity for learners to use a commentary to further explore the Letter of James. Individuals may choose to study either James 1:22-27 or James 2:8-13. Give each learner a commentary or make photocopies of the relevant pages to distribute. (Be sure to destroy all copies after the class to comply with copyright laws.) If time allows, learners might examine more than one commentary.

Direct the learners to see what answers they find in the commentary to the questions on the handout, "A Study of James." You may need to help youth use the commentaries if they are unfamiliar with the resource, but be sure to allow the youth to do as much of the work themselves as possible.

After the youth have done their work, discuss:
■ Do the commentaries help you understand the Scripture? If so, in what ways ?
■ Do you agree with the conclusions of the commentator? Why or why not?

OPTION B
Needed: Bibles, "Heroes Depicted in Movies and Books" handouts, writing utensils
James appears to have become quite vehement as he argued that works go hand in hand with faith. To drive home his point, he gave scriptural examples of two people who put faith into action: Abraham and Rahab.

If the youth are not familiar with these stories, they should look them up. James 2:21 refers to Abraham's willingness to sacrifice his son to God. Find the story in Genesis 22:1-14. James 2:25 refers to an episode from the Hebrew invasion of the Promised Land. Find that story in Joshua 2:1-21.

James cites these two very different individuals as examples of people who were justified (declared acceptable) to God because of their works. Ask:

■ Who can you cite as an example of faith in action similar to Abraham or Rahab?
■ Who do you know who has sacrificed a most precious thing or relationship in his or her life because God demanded it?
■ Who do you know who risked her or his security for the sake of a greater good?

The handout gives some examples of movies and books that deal with heroic acts. You might give some of these as between-session assignments to the youth. They should view or read their assignment and report to the group, comparing the heroism of the protagonists in these works to Abraham and Rahab.

**Living the Story
(15–20 minutes)**
OPTION A
(This option follows Option A of "Connecting to the Story.")
Needed: newsprint lists from "Connecting to the Story," newsprint and markers or chalkboard and chalk, Bibles, candle, matches or lighter
Break into the two subgroups used for Option A of "Connecting to the Story." Let the group choose a par-

ticular "orphan" or "widow" from their lists for whom they want to care. Share any appropriate information about this person.

The first act of care should be to pray for (1) God's guidance as you decide what to do, and (2) God's blessings on this person. Ask someone to pray out loud after the participants pray in silence for a period.

Begin a discussion about what to do by reading James 2:14-17. Write any and every idea on newsprint or chalkboard. For instance, say you chose an "orphan" whose parents are abusive. Ideas for help might range from "rescue by kidnapping" to "report to a school counselor." Next, discuss the practicality of doing each idea to narrow the list of possible actions (e.g., kidnapping is probably not a good idea!). Finally, vote on the ideas in order to choose one.

Plan ways to implement your action of care by setting specific goals as well as times and people who will be responsible for accomplishing those goals. After completing your plan, be sure to spend some time together debriefing and evaluating what you did.

Close by lighting a candle for this person and praying once again that God might guide you in your endeavor to care.

OPTION B
Needed: CD player, music CD as described below, copies of lyrics (on photocopies or newsprint), candle, matches or lighter, soft washcloths, bowls of warm water
Close by listening to a contemporary song about being a neighbor. "The Houseplant Song" by Audio

Adrenaline, from their *Underdog* album, is one option. You may know of another. Give everyone a copy of the lyrics to the song, or put them on newsprint ahead of time.

As the song plays, enter into a time of worship and meditation by lighting a candle and listening to the song. Play the song a second time. This time, wash one another's hands to symbolize the washing away of the stains of the world. Pair up and use soft washcloths dipped in warm water to wash each other's hands gently.

Conclude with a prayer of thanksgiving for God's great desire to enlist us in God's service.

Things to Ponder

Some of the youth may feel as if they are an "orphan" and may find those parts of this session's discussion difficult or moving. Be sure to follow up with any youth who seem to have struggled during the session or acted out in any way. You might also want to consider this session an opportunity to introduce youth to Christian music if they've not listened to it much before. There is some wonder-ful music out there in a variety of styles. Take the time to search out solid music to use in this session.

Looking Ahead

Depending on which options you choose, you may need to seek out a short story with some point about faith. Some suggested authors and resources are listed in the "You May Need" list for the next session.

Notes

1. "I Could Sing of Your Love Forever" can be found on the Delirious? CD entitled *Cutting Edge* (Chordant Distribution Group, 1997, ISBN 7474005301). It has also been recorded by other artists, such as Sonic Flood, and included on worship CD compilations. "Hands and Feet" can be found on the Audio Adrenaline CD entitled *Underdog* (Chordant Distribution Group, 1999, ISBN 747406409X). "El Salvador" can be found on the Phil Joel CD entitled *Watching Over You* (Chordant Distribution Group, 2000, ISBN 747410752X).

2. "The Houseplant Song" can be found on the Audio Adrenaline CD entitled *Underdog* (Chordant Distribution Group, 1999, ISBN 747406409X).

A Study of James

James 1:22-27

In James 1:22-27, what is "the perfect law" and "the law of liberty"?

To what does the word "blessed" refer in verse 25?

What might James say about a religion of devotional exercises?

Note other interesting findings.

James 2:8-13

In James 2:8-13, what is the "law of liberty"?

What is the meaning of "mercy triumphs over judgment"?

Where else in the Bible can you find the quotation in verse 8?

Note other interesting findings.

Heroes Depicted in Movies and Books

Movies | Synopsis

Pay It Forward
The story of a young boy who attempts to change the world with random acts of kindness.

Remember the Titans
A black football coach tries to work for the greater good under trying circumstances. Deals with the heroic acts of athletes challenged to become friends with "strangers."

O Brother, Where Art Thou?
Three escaped convicts experience many adventures and misadventures. They debate whether a higher power is at work in their lives while acting heroically to stay out of jail.

Schindler's List
A German acts at great risk to save Jews during WWII.

Family Man
Will a wealthy bachelor sacrifice his life of luxury to become a family man?

Proof of Life
A professional negotiator has second thoughts about abandoning a distraught wife whose husband has been kidnapped for ransom.

Books | Synopsis

The Chocolate War
by Robert Cormier
Laurel Leaf Library
Jerry Renault takes a stand at his school against the annual candy drive and suffers dire consequences.

The Giver
by Lois Lowry
Bantam Doubleday Dell Books
In a utopian world, Jonas is chosen to receive special training with The Giver—to take on all the memories of his society.

Heroes
by Robert Cormier
Laurel Leaf Library
Frances Joseph Cassavant, a war hero, returns home to kill his own childhood hero for mistreating the woman he loved.

In the Company of Angels
by N. M. Kelby
Hyperion
Two nuns risk much to rescue and protect a little French Jewish girl in WWII.

Many Stones
by Carolyn Coman
Front St. Press
Berry Morgan, estranged from her father, takes a trip with him to South Africa. There she encounters heroes of the anti-apartheid movement, leading to a rebirth.

The Ransom of Mercy Carter
by Caroline B. Cooney
Delacourt
Mercy Carter is captured by Indians in 1704. This is her heroic struggle to survive and even adapt to Indian culture while still thinking of herself as English.

The Terrorist
by Caroline B. Cooney
Delacourt
The heroic act of young Billy Williams results in his death. How will his family cope? Laura, a sister, is confronted with a situation that demands she take risks.

10. Joseph

Bible Story: Genesis 39:1-3; 45:1–46:7

Sandra DeMott Hasenauer

Salvation

A Story behind the Story

Before starting out, you might want to take the time to read the entire Joseph cycle (Genesis 37, 39–50). After all the events of the previous chapters, our session is focused on that section in which Joseph is confronted with his brothers' presence and must now make the decision as to how to proceed. Will he seek vengeance for their crimes of hate in the past, or will he forgive?

It is interesting to note in the story of Joseph something distinctly different from any other stories of the Hebrew patriarchs of the faith: we are never told of any direct conversations between God and Joseph. In fact, God remains quite behind the scenes throughout Joseph's entire story. On occasion, Joseph's story is highlighted by conversations between God and Jacob, but there are no direct theophanies (appearances of God) to Joseph himself. Perhaps this detail makes Joseph's story all the more close to our own—most of us have never had God appear directly to us. Rather, we are called upon to find God in daily events of life, seeing God's face in the people around us and trusting to our own faith and sense of God's will to direct us.

We are told that the Lord was with Joseph (Genesis 39:3) and caused him to prosper. Joseph's own understanding of his life's events were firmly rooted in his faith as well, as he tells his brothers, "It was not you who sent me here, but God" (Genesis 45:8). Despite the lack of direct contact from God throughout the story, it conveys an undisputed understanding of God's purpose and will at work.

Not altogether unrelated, however, is a second point to be made about the Joseph story: this is a tale of power, used and abused. From dysfunctional family to royal court, we get a feel for the world's power versus God's power. God may either take advantage of the world's power or subvert it completely—in either case, God is determined to have the divine will realized. Perhaps, for youth who are just beginning to experience their own sense of personal power or are wondering if they have any power at all, this might be the strongest sense of connection with the story. It is for this reason that the steps below follow a sequence to help youth with the exploration of power in the story. (Other sessions have options that may be mixed and matched to some extent. In this session, you will find it most effective to choose all Option A's or all Option B's as you move through the lesson.)

Enter the Story

As mentioned above, it would be helpful if you took the time to read the entire Joseph cycle in order to properly frame this story. (Your youth will need a similar orientation to the larger story, so take notes as you read, in preparation for summarizing the background for the group later.)

- Where is God at work in the events of my own life?
- How can I forgive my family for wrongs I think they've done to me?
- What wrongs might I have done to my family or myself?
- I have no power. How can God use me?

YOU MAY NEED

- Bibles
- newsprint
- markers
- short story (or excerpt) about faith
- props or costumes as available
- a video of the Joseph story, possibly even a children's cartoon version
- TV and VCR
- paper
- writing utensils
- CD player and CD of soft background music (optional)
- "Power to the People" handouts
- "God's Ways" handouts
- 3″ x 5″ index cards

Get comfortable, find your favorite translation, put on some soft music, and perhaps light a candle. It is a wonderful story that deserves your undivided attention. Before and after reading it, pray that God's will for you might become clear through your study.

Setting the Stage
(5–10 minutes)
OPTION A
Needed: newsprint, markers
Welcome the youth to the room and begin with whatever opening ritual you may have developed together as a class. Be sure to check in with the youth as to the events of their lives during the time between your last session and this. Consider especially focusing on family issues: How are their family members? Any memorable family events this week? You will need to do this with some sensitivity, as some youth might have different "family" definitions than others.

After you've spent a few moments checking in, invite the youth to respond to the following question: *Who in our society has power?* Write their responses on newsprint as they are offered. Name some specific people in the United States today whom you consider powerful. Refrain from defining "power" for the youth at this point—simply get them to name some so-called powerful people.

After they have a list, ask: *What is it that makes these people powerful?* If appropriate, write specific responses next to the appropriate names, such as "fame" next to "Britney Spears." Finally, after the youth have spent some time consid-

ering that question, suggest that today's story has to do with a young man who ended up with an awful lot of power.

OPTION B
Needed: short story of faith
After the youth have arrived, ask whether any of them has ever actually seen God face-to-face or heard God's voice. Chances are, they'll say they haven't! Suggest that most of us who try to do so can discover God in the day-to-day, in the events of our lives and the people around us.

Invite the group to get comfortable; then begin with this quotation by Frederick Buechner: *"It seemed to me then, and seems to me still, that if God speaks to us at all in this world, if God speaks anywhere, it is into our personal lives that he speaks. . . . Into the thick of it, or out of the thick of it, at moments of even the most humdrum of our days, God speaks."*[1]

Share with the group a short story of faith that you've found, one that illustrates how God is at work in our lives, one that can be read aloud in about five minutes.[2] You might also excerpt part of a longer story. After the story is over, explain that today's Scripture story is a tale of God at work in the events of one person's life.

Telling the Story
(5–10 minutes)
Needed: video of Joseph story (optional), TV and VCR (optional), Bibles, props or costumes (optional)
Since this session's Scripture picks up toward the end of Joseph's story

with his brothers and enslavement in Egypt, most likely you will have to fill the class in on the details. If you have one, use a video version of Joseph's story to help fill the youth in on the details of his life prior to this session's Scripture portion. Do not be afraid to use a children's cartoon version; often youth enjoy watching these as a return-to-childhood kind of thing. One suggestion might be *The Beginner's Bible: The Story of Joseph and His Brothers* (Sony VHS, Beginner's Bible video series, 1999). Make sure the video is brief, as you will need time to read the Scripture as well (obviously, you will only need to show the part that leads up to this Scripture).

In lieu of a video, offer a verbal summary of the background to the session's Scripture story. You will want to keep this summary brief, but make sure the pertinent details are covered. Who was Joseph, how did he get enslaved, and how did he end up being prime minister? As suggested above, prepare this summary in advance so that you hit all the high points without taking too much time on the background.

The Bible story itself for this session is a rather long passage for youth to hear in one sitting, so consider reading the story with characters as follows: narrator, Joseph, Pharaoh, Pharaoh's servant (45:16), Joseph's brothers, Jacob/Israel, God's voice. Ask for volunteers to read each of these parts as you come to them, with one person serving as the narrator who reads the remainder of the parts. If you choose, you might even want to have the youth act

it out as you go, using props or costumes that you might have readily available in the room.

Reacting to the Story (10–15 minutes)

OPTION A

Invite the youth to break into pairs or triads to discuss the following questions. Allow time between each question for discussion.

■ How do you think Joseph felt toward his brothers when he was in the pit? When he was sold to slavers? In Egypt, once he'd been made the equivalent of a prime minister?

■ How do you think he was able to forgive his brothers?

■ Would you have been able to forgive them, if you were Joseph? Why or why not?

■ Have you ever had to forgive someone? Was it hard? Why or why not?

OPTION B
(This option follows Option B of "Setting the Stage.")
Needed: paper, writing utensils, CD player and CD
Make sure the youth have writing paper and writing utensils. Remind them of the story you read in Option B of "Setting the Stage." Suggest that sometimes the best way for us to explain our faith is simply to tell stories. If someone asks us, "Do you believe in God?" and we say, "Yes," the other's next question might be "Why?" Many times, we respond to that "why" not with a laundry list of reasons but with a story. For example, "I believe in God because when my grandmother passed away. . . ."

Invite class members to separate themselves from each other for privacy and diminished distraction; then instruct them to take several minutes to consider a time when God might have been at work in the events of their life. Invite them to write about that time. If they choose, they could create a poem or fictional story along the same lines. Suggest that if they aren't sure God has ever been at work in their life, they might consider writing about that issue in story or poetry form.

Play some soft music in the background while the youth do their work. After they are finished writing (or you've called time), invite volunteers to share. However, respect individuals' need for privacy, and do not force anyone to share.

Connecting to the Story (10–15 minutes)

OPTION A
(This option follows Option A of "Setting the Stage.")
Needed: "Power to the People" handouts, writing utensils, Bibles
Give a copy of the "Power to the People" handout and a writing utensil to each youth. Break into small groups, pairs, or triads (whichever format is most comfortable and effective). Make sure each small group has at least one Bible.

You may want to explain that the Scriptures listed on the handout go outside of the Scriptures that are central to this session, but they are important to understanding the flow of the Joseph story. Therefore, they are important to understanding the particular Scriptures of this session. (You might also want to

suggest that the youth refrain from reading the longer Scriptures out loud—this tends to take longer.)

Invite the youth to work together to complete Part I. After they've done the chart, they should respond to the "arrowed" questions either as a group or individually, whichever is appropriate to the particular question. After they've done so, invite the small groups to share their responses with the class as a whole (including the arrowed questions, as they may be comfortable doing so).

OPTION B
Needed: "God's Ways" handouts, writing utensils, Bibles
Give each youth a copy of the "God's Ways" handout and a writing utensil. Invite the youth to read the instructions and complete the handout. Suggest that they read through all of the statements before responding to any of them, as some of the statements contradict each other. Also remind them that this work is as private as they choose to make it. Although they will have an opportunity to share their responses with others, they need not do so if they are uncomfortable with it. Also explain that all of the statements on the handout are those that might be expressed by different Christians. People have different experiences of God, whether or not we personally agree with them. This experience is to help the youth determine what they might believe about God's relationship with the world at this time.

After they've had a chance to note their responses, have the group get into pairs or triads to discuss their handouts; then invite one volunteer to read Isaiah 55:8-11 and another to read Romans 8:28, to the whole class. Have the youth compare what they hear in these Scriptures with their responses on the handouts. Discuss in small groups:

■ What are the similarities?
■ Do the Scriptures bring you any comfort? Why or why not?

**Exploring the Story
(10–15 minutes)**
OPTION A
(This option follows Option A of "Connecting to the Story.")
Needed: "Power to the People" handouts, writing utensils, Bibles
Draw the class's attention to Part II of the "Power to the People" handout. If your class is larger, consider breaking into pairs or triads for this step. Otherwise, invite youth to work on their own. In this step, youth will be exploring further the concept of power in the Joseph cycle and what the story might have to teach us about the proper use of power.

After the youth have finished working on Part II, invite a volunteer to read Mark 10:41-45. Have the group compare this teaching of Jesus' with the study of power they've done. Do they see an example of it in the Joseph story?

OPTION B
Needed: Bibles
Explain that some scholars have pointed out that the Joseph cycle at some of its most significant points compares with the story of Jesus' life, death, and resurrection—if you read Joseph metaphorically, that is.

At the top of a large piece of newsprint, write the names "Jesus" and "Joseph" side by side, drawing a vertical line between them to divide the paper in half. Depending on how intuitive you think your group is, you may want to start things off by writing on the far left side such categories as:
■ God speaks to/about
■ Death
■ Resurrection
Have the youth review the highlights of Jesus' life and death, making reference to whichever Gospel you prefer. Draw the group's attention in particular to the Passion story and to what God says to and about Jesus. Fill in the left column with things such as "He was God's beloved son," "He fed hungry people," "His disciples abandoned him," "He was killed," and "He was resurrected."

Now invite the youth to consider the story of Joseph (going outside of this session's Scripture for the background to the story), filling in the right column under his name with brief descriptions that parallel Jesus' life. Remember: think about the Joseph story metaphorically. For instance, Joseph isn't killed at any time in the story, but someone thinks he's dead. He is not resurrected, but he does "come back to life" for someone. Joseph isn't called God's beloved son, but he was Jacob's favorite. We are not told that God speaks directly to Joseph, but he does have visions. As the exercise progresses, the youth may discover additional parallels to Jesus' life by looking more closely at Joseph's.

83

Once the newsprint is complete, ask the youth to discuss: *What is God's plan for us, based on these two stories? In other words, what can these two stories tell us about the nature of God and about God's relationship with us?*

Living the Story (5–10 minutes)
OPTION A
(This option continues the Option A sequence of previous steps.)
Needed: "Power to the People" handouts, writing utensils
Again draw the class's attention to the "Power to the People" handout. Explain that teenagers often feel completely powerless to do anything about the world and the circumstances that surround us. Suggest that most adults often feel the same way! It is hard to imagine that we can have any effect on the world. However, today's story shows us that God is able to use anyone to affect the world, if we remain open and attuned to God's will. Invite youth to complete Part III of the handout on their own, reminding them to be respectful of each other's privacy and to refrain from distracting each other. Give them sufficient time for their reflection and then bring them back together.

Reminding them that changing the world begins at home, invite the youth to consider how their relationships with family and friends might have more far-reaching effects. How might using their power of relationship for good with a friend affect that friend or other people that friend

might meet years down the road? How might it affect they themselves in the future?

After you've had a few minutes of discussion, gather together for a time of closing prayer. Be sure to ask God to help the group to become aware of your own power for harm and good. Ask also for God's guidance in using that power wisely.

OPTION B
Needed: index cards, writing utensils
Hand out an index card and writing utensil to each youth. Remind the group of Joseph's forgiveness of his brothers in today's Scripture story. The brothers' minds were still in the past—they remembered what they had done to Joseph and were afraid that was all he could remember as well. However, Joseph's response was based in the present. He found himself able to forgive their actions in the past and move on.

God's response to us is also not dependent upon our past. God wants us now, and God wants to move with us into the future.

Read verses 11 and 25 of Isaiah 43 to the class. Invite the youth to write on their index cards either something for which they'd like to ask God's forgiveness or a prayer for God's forgiveness. They are to keep these private. After they've done so, gather in a circle and lead the group in prayer, leaving a time of silence in the middle for the youth to offer their own prayers seeking God's forgiveness (either silently or aloud).

Things to Ponder

Some youth come from families where the actions of Joseph's brothers may not feel so foreign, so be sensitive to these kinds of situations when dealing with the story. Follow up the session with notes of encouragement where you may feel it is appropriate.

Looking Ahead

If you choose Option A of "Telling the Story," you will need to plan out a route of travel through the church ahead of time and set up props in certain places. Be sure, as you're doing your planning, to take into account where other classes might be meeting so that you do not disturb anyone else. You may also need to find a recording of the spiritual "Deep River." Suggestions for this are listed in the "You May Need" section.

Notes

1. Some good authors to explore are Frederick Buechner, Walter Wangerin, Maya Angelou (particularly her autobiographical works), and Henri J. M. Nouwen. If you're unfamiliar with these authors, it might be best to find one of the daily devotional books that contain excerpts of their works, such as *Listening to Your Life: Daily Meditations with Frederick Buechner* (San Francisco: HarperSanFrancisco, 1992), *Measuring the Days: Daily Reflections with Walter Wangerin, Jr.* (San Francisco: HarperSanFrancisco, 1993), or Nouwen's *Can You Drink the Cup?* (Notre Dame, Ind.: Ave Maria Press, 1996).
2. Frederick Buechner, *The Sacred Journey: A Memoir of Early Days* (San Francisco: HarperSanFrancisco, 1982), pp. 1–2.

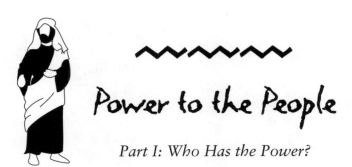

Power to the People

Part I: Who Has the Power?

In the following segments of the story, note the names of the people who have power and the people who do not have power.

	Powerful	Powerless	Why?
Genesis 37:1-4			
Genesis 37:5-11			
Genesis 37:14b-24			
Genesis 37:25-28			
Genesis 39:1			
Genesis 39:2-3			
Genesis 39:19-20			
Genesis 39:21-23			
Genesis 41:14-43			
Genesis 42:6-17			
Genesis 45:1-16			

➡ When is the power in the story different from what you might normally expect?

➡ Why does that happen?

➡ To which character do you relate best: Joseph? Pharaoh? One of the brothers? Why?

Part II: What Is Power?

1. Looking at the chart above, list here who had power at any given time in the story. Leave room beside each name for more notes.

2. What kind of power did each person have? Consider these three definitions: *Political power* is that kind which is granted based on an office held. *Social power* is that granted to you based on things generally beyond your control: birth order, gender, economic status, etc. Let's call the third type *power of faith,* that kind which is granted to a person by God. On the list above, indicate which category you think each person fell into. (Consider whether they might fall into more than one category.)

3. In the story, power might have been used well or it might have been abused (to harm someone or get one's own way). Sometimes the same character used or abused power in different parts of the story. On the list you just made, write next to each character's name "used well" or "abused" to indicate how you feel they used their power. If it changed in different parts of the story, write both next to the name.

4. Finally, the story mentions that God used all of these events to work out the divine will. With the same list above, write "used" if you think God used the power already present with or in the person or their office. Or write "subvert" if you think God reversed the normal power and made the opposite happen than what we might expect.

Part III: Do I Have Power?

➡ It might not feel like it, but we all have some kind of power. For example, are you the officer of any clubs? Do you have any friends? Do you have any brothers or sisters? Do you have parents? Are you physically strong? Are you good with words? All of these things give you power—the power of decision making, the power of hurt, the power of skill or talent, the power of relationship. List here (and be honest) what kinds of power you have.

➡ For each item on the above list, consider how you could use that power for good rather than harm. Choose one that you feel is most significant or necessary for you to work on right now, and write below what the power is, with whom you have that power, and how you might use it for good. Be specific!

God's Ways

Rate your responses to the following statements on this spectrum:

1 = disagree strongly
2 = somewhat disagree
3 = neutral
4 = somewhat agree
5 = agree strongly

1	2	3	4	5

God moves in mysterious ways.

1	2	3	4	5

Everything that happens has a purpose.

1	2	3	4	5

God is always in control.

1	2	3	4	5

Some things "just happen." God may not control them, but God finds a way to use them.

1	2	3	4	5

God created the world, but God doesn't try to change things now. God is like a clockmaker who makes a clock and then just watches it run on its own.

1	2	3	4	5

If I pray hard enough, I can figure out what God wants me to do.

1	2	3	4	5

Decisions I make have an effect on whether or not God's will for the world can be carried out.

11. Joshua

Bible Story: Joshua 3–4

Sandra DeMott Hasenauer

A Story behind the Story

"So that all the peoples of the earth may know that the hand of the Lord is mighty, and so that you may fear the Lord your God forever" (Joshua 4:24).

Imagine if the entire history of the world were written by one person who wanted to make a point. What might that historical text look like? What would it include? What might it leave out? It's actually not hard to imagine; one has only to go to the nearest bookstore to see shelves of historical texts written by historians with a theory. There is no such thing as objective history—we all see history through certain lenses. The Deuteronomic historian is no different.

Most scholars agree that the bulk of the Pentateuch (Genesis through Deuteronomy) and several of the later historical books of the Bible were probably edited and compiled by one person or by a group of people who shared a single school of thought. This person (or group) is often referred to as the Deuteronomic historian. The editor brought together a loose collection of stories that had grown up and lived through generations of oral telling, then put them in one place in a particular order. The stories were about a relationship—a relationship between a single God and that God's chosen people. The stories were about an experience—the experience of the power and wisdom of God discovered through the events of history. This was pretty progressive for the time; most other peoples were worshiping multiple deities. But Israel's God was one entity. The one God; the God of Abraham, Isaac, and Jacob; the God of Creation, of the Flood, and of the Exodus—this was the God of a salvation played out in history.

The Book of Joshua is an overview of the conquest and occupation of the Promised Land. This book is a sequel of sorts to the Pentateuch. Its stories show the fulfillment of the promises God made to Abraham and Moses in Genesis and Exodus. But the sequel is written with a point: the prosperity of God's chosen people depended completely on whether or not they obeyed God's commands. When they did, things went well for them. When they were disobedient, well . . . the stories of Joshua are quite clear on that point.

This session deals with the actual crossing of the Jordan into the Promised Land. The sequel has begun.

Enter the Story

If you get the chance, consider reading the whole of the Book of Joshua prior to working on this session's particular passage. The book contains stories that can be difficult to stomach. How do we square the conquering God with the inclusive God? How do we understand these stories and integrate them into our faith? Pray as you read the Scripture for this session, asking for God's guidance to go before you much like the ark went before the Israelites.

POSSIBLE YOUTH CONTACT POINTS

- Where is God?
- How do I know God is leading me?
- Can I rely on God?

YOU MAY NEED

- newsprint
- markers
- Bibles
- writing utensils, including ballpoint pens
- twelve stones, larger than softball size if possible
- object to represent the ark of the covenant
- one rock (any size will do)
- "Promises, Promises" handouts
- variety of props (optional)
- video camera, TV, and VCR (optional)
- craft supplies, such as cardboard boxes, masking tape, gold wrapping or tissue paper, pipe cleaners, cardboard tubes, dowel rods, paints, thick markers, duct tape
- "Crossing the Jordan" handouts
- Bible concordances
- hymnals
- CD recording of "Deep River"
- CD player
- inexpensive washcloths
- index cards

Setting the Stage
(5–10 minutes)
OPTION A

After the youth have arrived, you've greeted them, and you've spent a few minutes checking in with them about the events of their lives, ask them if they've seen any good sequels lately at the movies. Make sure they know what a sequel is— a book or movie that continues a story begun in a preceding one. Sequels that have multiple installments might be called "trilogies" (with three installments, such as the *Lord of the Rings* trilogy) or "series" (such as the C. S. Lewis *Narnia* series). Invite them to name some sequels that have come out recently. (Most likely these will be movies, but they might be books or even "concept albums.") What do they like about sequels? What do they dislike?

After a few minutes of discussion, explain that today's Scripture story is itself a sequel of sorts.

OPTION B

After the youth have arrived, spend a few minutes checking in with them. Allow for a little storytelling. If you can, casually tell a story of your own about getting lost or trying to follow vague directions. You might even want to take the liberty of telling an old story as if it happened in the last few days, so that it feels less contrived. Keep the story fairly brief and casual, and see if it sparks (naturally) other like stories from the youth.

After a few moments, pretend to suddenly remember something you've forgotten. Ask one of the youth to get something for you,

but give that young person no direction. For example, say, "James, I need the star. Please go get it for me." If the person asks where or how, say, "I don't know. I just need it. Please get it."

Keep it going for a minute or two. If you have a small building, allow the youth you've asked to find the object to leave the room in search of it. But make sure you will be able to call him or her back into the room without losing a lot of time finding this person!

Once you've had a bit of conversation about trying to find something without directions, discuss:
- How hard is it to go somewhere without any directions?
- Do you get lost?

Inform the youth that part of the story for today includes God giving directions and guiding the way for the Israelites. Ask: *How do you seek God's directions?*

Telling the Story
(5–10 minutes)
OPTION A

Needed: Bibles, twelve stones, object to represent the ark of the covenant

This story is a very mobile one, with lots of movement and travel involved. Take advantage of that in the telling of the story. Ahead of time, consider a course through your church building that might approximate the course taken by the Israelites in these two chapters from Joshua (being sure that you won't disturb any other classes in session). Where would Shittim be? The Jordan? The camp on either side of the Jordan (the later one at Gilgal)? The dry spot in the middle of the

Jordan? Wherever you determine the dry spot in the middle of the Jordan to be, lay down twelve stones ahead of time. In the classroom, leave something large (e.g., cardboard box, folding chair) that will represent the ark of the covenant to be carried by some of the youth throughout the reading of the story.

When it's time to read the Scripture, assign some of the youth to be the Levitical priests, whose task it is to carry the ark. Make sure the rest have their Bibles with them. Read the story in whatever form you choose: you can read it yourself, with everyone else following along, or you can have volunteers read sections. In either case, move through your chosen "route" as you read, acting out such things as the ark moving into the middle of the Jordan ahead of the people, the twelve stones being taken from the center of the river and placed as a testimony to the events, etc. Be sure to have the people walk two thousand cubits behind the ark (approximately a thousand feet, although you'll probably need to fudge this with something more realistic).

Note: consider having "Gilgal" as your classroom. That way, you will naturally be back in the right spot to finish the session.

OPTION B
Needed: Bibles, one rock
Explain to the youth that in the Old Testament rocks often stand as witness to the works of God. Suggest that today, for us, the words of Scripture stand as witness to the works of God. Invite the youth to read the Scripture story, passing the rock among them to indicate who is

to read next. While holding the rock, each person will read his or her section and then pass the rock to the next person to read.

Reacting to the Story (10–15 minutes)
OPTION A
Needed: Bibles, "Promises, Promises" handouts, writing utensils
Make sure each youth has a Bible, and give them each a copy of the "Promises, Promises" handout and a writing utensil. Instruct them to take several minutes to go through the handout on their own, filling it out as best they can by themselves.

Make sure they understand that they have to think through how the promises might be interpreted in the story. The word *promise* never actually shows up in the Scripture itself (at least not in the NRSV version). Ask: *What promises are explicit in the story? Which might be just implied?* Ask youth to imagine what might have happened if the promises were broken.

Once they have completed the handout on their own, have them get together in twos or threes and share their responses.

After they've spent some time considering the story, have them share a time when someone broke a promise to them or they broke a promise themselves. Ask:
■ What was the promise? Was it a positive promise or a negative one?
■ How did it feel to have that promise broken?
■ Do you know people who are always making promises and breaking them? How much do you trust that person?

After they've spent some time discussing these things, invite them to consider God's promises. Ask: *Can we trust God's promises? Why or why not? What do stories like this one about Joshua teach us about God and promises?*

OPTION B
Needed: large stones (one per person), markers
Give each youth a stone, explaining (if you haven't already) that in the Old Testament stones often stand as witness to the works of God. Remind the youth of the last part of the Scripture story, in which Joshua sets up the twelve stones and explains why he is doing so (Joshua 4:19-24). Invite the youth to write on their stone words or phrases that jumped out at them from the reading of the story. These might be overall themes that they heard, particular words that meant something to them, or even something they question about the story.

After they've done this, invite them to share with a partner what they have written on their stones, and why. Once they've done this, have the youth pile their stones in the middle of the room, and suggest that these rocks now also stand in this room as a witness to God's work.

**Connecting to the Story
(10–15 minutes)**
OPTION A
Needed: Bibles, variety of props (optional), video camera, TV, and VCR (optional)
Note that the Book of Joshua is considered a sequel to Genesis and Exodus. In some respects, the three

books might be considered a trilogy about God's relationship with the chosen people and the formation of that people into a nation. Have the youth consider other movie trilogies they've seen. Invite them to remember the trailers they saw for those movies (the trailers being the advertisements for one movie that are shown at the beginning of a different movie).

Next, have the youth break into smaller groups of about four to six people each. Invite each group to come up with a "movie trailer" for a trilogy of movies based on Genesis, Exodus, and Joshua. Encourage them to see if they can somehow make an overarching theme of the stories explicit in their trailer. They will also want to check their Bibles for significant events that might be included in these "films." If possible, make props and costuming available. Allow time for the small groups to perform their trailers for each other. Consider videotaping their trailers and showing them afterward.

OPTION B
Needed: Bibles, craft supplies
Point out to the youth the passages that refer to the ark of the covenant. Ask:
■ What did this ark symbolize to the people?
■ Why do you think they had to stand so far away from it?
■ Why might it have been important to have it go into the water first?
■ What purpose did the ark serve in the crossing of the Jordan?

After the discussion, inform the class that you, as a group, are now going to create your own ark of the covenant. Provide them with craft supplies (see list under "You May Need") and invite them to check Exodus 37:1-9 for a description of the ark. Remind them to leave space in their decorating for them to write on it later. Also remind them to leave an opening on top.

After they have constructed their ark, tell the youth that just as the ark guided the Israelites across the Jordan, so God still guides us through the difficulties in our lives. Invite the youth to consider ways in which God provides guidance to them in their lives and, using markers, to write words or phrases that describe those ways on the side of the ark. After they've done so, put the ark in the front of the classroom for use later.

Exploring the Story (10–15 minutes)

OPTION A

Remind the group that the Old Testament is the story of a people's experience of God through the events of history. They interpret the events they live through in the light of their faith in God. Sometimes this interpretation is in their favor and sometimes it is not (that is, they interpret their own prosperity or failure based on their relationship with God). We may or may not agree with these interpretations of historical events, but the fact of the matter is, most of us do not receive direct visions from God and have to rely on the world around us to give us our experience of God.

Invite the youth to come up with a recent event in history ("history" can be yesterday) and discuss how

God might have been revealed through that event. Be careful to encourage respect for differing opinions—there are no "right" answers for this type of discussion. Allow yourself enough time for a really good discussion, and feel free to have the youth work with two or three different events in succession. If you do so, try to have them come up with events of different categories, such as "natural events" (earthquakes, hurricanes, etc.), "human events" (events precipitated by human action), "scientific events" (such as space launches, recent discoveries), and so on.

OPTION B

Needed: newsprint, markers, "Crossing the Jordan" handouts, Bibles, concordances, hymnals, CD recording of "Deep River," CD player

Inform the class that the river Jordan has taken on a life of its own in Christian experience. Make available concordances and Bibles and have the youth look up the references to the Jordan in the Bible. They should note what happens in each instance it is mentioned.

After they've done so, see if they can figure out different things the Jordan might have come to symbolize to Christians through the years. Discuss these possibilities as a class, writing them on newsprint. Give the youth the "Crossing the Jordan" handout and invite them to complete it, sharing their responses as a class afterward. Play the recording of "Deep River,"[1] and have the youth look through the hymnals for any references to the Jordan.

Are any of them familiar? Refer to the list you made previously of what the Jordan symbolizes. Do they have any additions or changes they might make to the list now?

Living the Story
(5–10 minutes)
OPTION A
Needed: washcloths, Bibles, ballpoint pens
Read to the class Joshua 3:5. Discuss with the youth what it might mean to "sanctify" yourself.

Some faith traditions have linked this with purification ceremonies that involve physical bathing along with prayers. Others use incense or smoke. Have the youth imagine what they might do to symbolize sanctifying themselves, guiding the discussion with such questions as the following:

■ What symbolic elements might sanctification include?
■ What physical acts might be involved?
■ Why would Joshua tell the people to sanctify themselves before God could do wonders among them?
■ What link is there between sanctification and God's ability to move among us, if any?

As always, there are not any right answers here; encourage the youth to do their own interpretation.

After you've had some discussion, give each youth a washcloth and a pen. (If you have a large group, you might cut the washcloths into pieces and distribute those to the youth.) Invite the youth to write on their washcloth a prayer asking God to help them to be ready for God to work won-

ders in their lives. Close with a time of prayer together.

OPTION B
(Use this option if you chose Option B of "Connecting to the Story.")
Needed: ark of the covenant (created earlier in this session), index cards, writing utensils, CD player and CD of "Deep River"
Have the youth gather in a seated circle, and move the ark they made into the center. Read Joshua 3:1-3a (ending with "before") to the youth, and remind them that the ark is a symbol of God's guidance to a wandering people. Hand out the index cards and writing utensils. Invite the youth to consider where in their life they might feel lost and in need of God's help to find direction. Consider playing a recording of the spiritual "Deep River" in the background, especially if it is Paul Robeson's version or a quiet, instrumental version.

After the youth have had some time to think, instruct them to write a prayer on their index cards, lifting up their area of lostness to God and inviting God's guidance and wisdom.

When everyone has finished, stand and join hands and share in a time of prayer together. Open the time of prayer with an invitation for the youth to either read their written prayer aloud when it comes their turn or remain in silence. In either case, the youth should then place their index cards into the ark. Begin the prayer yourself, and then indicate with a squeeze of the hand when the next person should pray. Close the time of prayer together by saying the Lord's Prayer in unison.

Things to Ponder

There are several points in this session in which the youth's personal experience might have tremendous impact upon the way they "hear" the Scripture: when mentioning racial issues, during conversations of lostness, while discussing broken promises, etc. Be aware of each youth and the way he or she is responding to different parts of the lesson, and be prepared to follow up as might be necessary later.

Looking Ahead

Depending on which options you choose, you may need to find an adult volunteer (whose role is described in the next session under "Setting the Stage") from an adult class or from a board or committee of the church. You may also need to bring a name definition book, such as a baby name book or other resource.

Note

1. The song "Deep River" can be found on several of Paul Robeson's CDs, although *Ballad for Americans* (Vanguard Records, rereleased 1991) is specifically mentioned on the handout. If you'd like quiet instrumental music, try Charlie Miller, *Melodies from the Heart* (Orchard Records, 2000), for a medley of "Jordan" songs, including "Deep River," on solo piano. Other artists who have recorded the song include Marian Anderson, Leontyne Price, the Mormon Tabernacle Choir, Odetta, and Jimmy Witherspoon. There are also many jazz and blues versions available.

Promises, Promises

Read through Joshua 3–4, looking for the following things. There may be more than one answer for each, and the answer might not be immediately clear. You'll need to think broadly for this and, in some cases, use your imagination!

WHO makes a promise?	TO WHOM is the promise made?	WHAT is the promise?	WHAT IS NEEDED for the promise to work?	WHAT HAPPENS if the promise is broken?

Crossing the Jordan

Paul Robeson's dad was born a slave. At age fifteen, however, he escaped slavery, eventually studying theology and becoming a preacher. Paul's mother was a teacher, but she died when Paul was only six.

Paul, born in 1898, grew up as one of only two black students in his high school in New Jersey in the early 1900s, when racism was rampant. Despite this, he acted in stage dramas (having the lead in Shakespeare's *Othello*), sang in the choir, and played football. He excelled at athletics, singing, and academics, graduating with honors. In fact, he won a scholarship to Rutgers University. He was an All-American football player at the same time that he achieved significant academic success.

In the early 1920s he was studying law at Columbia University and playing professional football on the weekends. After graduation, he took a job with a law firm in New York. However, when a white stenographer in the firm refused to take dictation from him because he was black, Robeson realized that this response was indicative of the attitude toward his race in the law in general, and he left the field. His wife then encouraged him to return to his acting and singing, and so he joined an acting troupe.

Robeson enjoyed tremendous success on the stage all over the world, primarily as a solo vocalist. Despite his fame worldwide, however, in the United States there were still restaurants in which he could not eat, his audiences were segregated because blacks were not allowed certain seats, and his performances invited threats and harassment because he was black. While traveling, he developed a tremendous appreciation for the peoples of the world, learning no fewer than twenty-five languages. Robeson became a political activist throughout the 1930s and 1940s, working for civil rights, economic justice, and the political inclusion of all people the world over. He saw his singing as a vehicle for education about racial justice, working folk songs from many countries into his vocal repertoire, including the spirituals of slaves.

On his album entitled *Ballad for Americans* (among others), Robeson recorded the slave spiritual "Deep River." It includes the following words:

Deep river, my home is over Jordan.
Deep river, Lord, I want to cross over into campground.

1. Why do you think the story of crossing the Jordan River into the Promised Land appealed to slaves?

2. Why do you think Robeson was careful to include this song on this album recorded in the 1950s?

3. The Underground Railroad often used spirituals as "code language" for getting information, warnings, and other messages through to slaves. The river Jordan sometimes referred to the Ohio River, the crossing of which would put slaves into abolitionist states. Why do you think slaves linked crossing the Ohio River with the crossing of the Jordan in Joshua?

4. Why do you think Jesus was baptized in the Jordan River? What kind of link might there be between the story of Jesus' baptism and the story in Joshua?

5. How would you define the word *salvation*? What does it mean in our faith? What do you think this story of the crossing of the Jordan has to do with our understanding of salvation?

12. Abigail

Bible Story: 1 Samuel 25

Sandra DeMott Hasenauer

A Story behind the Story

When read with modern eyes, this story raises disturbing questions, such as, How can Abigail just run off and happily marry a man she's met for presumably about ten minutes, so quickly after her husband drops dead of natural (or supernatural) causes? However, the romance is almost beside the point here, other than to further solidify David's rise to kingship. Rather, this story is one of revenge averted, the significance of names, and clever women.

It has been said that Abigail is almost a personification of the "wise woman" of Proverbs 31, an image central to the Israelite wisdom tradition. Her literary foil—in this case, Nabal—is the "foolish man." We are told straight out in the story in 1 Samuel 25 that Nabal's name means "foolish" (verse 25), whereas Abigail's name in Hebrew means "my father rejoices."

Nabal, apparently, was lucky to have a wife who was more savvy in interpersonal relations than he himself was. Abigail went to great trouble to smooth over the impending dispute between her husband and the stranger.

Did she truly have some foreknowledge of who David was and would become, or was she simply acting out of the culture of hospitality that existed in those times? We don't know. Her statements in verse 28, which seem to predict David's eventual greatness, should not necessarily be taken as prophecy on her part. It might be seen simply as a way of assuaging a potentially dangerous army captain's ego, or it might also be a later addition by the person who put the story in writing. On the other hand, sometimes we say things that are unwittingly predictive. Abigail's words, read now centuries later, certainly act as prophecy for us. We know that Abigail was taking the wiser part, because we know "the end of the story," as it were. However, when looking at the story, we should be careful to look at it from the point of view of "then" as well as "now."

How great a risk did Abigail take, approaching David as she did? And what about possible retribution from this nasty character she's married to? Just how much did she accomplish by her actions? What does this story have to tell us about temper and revenge? This story offers several valuable avenues of inquiry, and the youth will have the opportunity to explore as they may choose.

Enter the Story

If you have the time, consider reading the entirety of 1 Samuel, especially the stories that bracket the story for this session (chapters 24 and 26). This story is part of a minicycle of biblical stories that show David's opportunities for revenge and his reactions to the situation. Consider your own feelings about getting even, pray for God's guidance as you explore these issues, and then settle down with your favorite Bible for a good read.

POSSIBLE YOUTH CONTACT POINTS

- Is "getting even" right or wrong?
- How can I show thanks to God?
- Have I ever had to smooth things over with someone?
- Can I live up to people's expectations of me?

YOU MAY NEED

- party decorations
- party music (optional)
- snacks
- adult volunteer
- costuming and props (optional)
- Bibles
- newsprint and markers (optional)
- "What's in a Name?" handout
- writing utensils
- name definition books (such as baby name books)
- Bible study aids such as study Bible, dictionaries, encyclopedias, commentaries
- "Exploration Points" handouts
- candle
- matches or lighter
- CD of quiet background music
- CD player

Setting the Stage
(5–10 minutes)
OPTION A

Needed: party decorations, party music and CD player (optional), plentiful snacks, adult volunteer

Prior to the session, find a volunteer from an adult education class or some other adult group in the church who would be willing to participate in this step. Work out some prearranged timing between the two of you for when the person should interrupt your group.

On the day of the session, set up your meeting room as if for a big party: streamers, balloons, a table laden with snacks, maybe some party music. Specifically, make sure you have plenty of snacks—far more than enough for everyone.

As the youth arrive, welcome them to the party. Make up any excuse you want for having the party: Is it near some birthdays? Are you celebrating the color blue? The reason doesn't matter—simply set a festive atmosphere.

Once everyone has arrived and your party is in full swing, have the adult volunteer interrupt your class and say something similar to what David said to Nabal, only updating it for your church. Perhaps she or he could say, "What a great party you're having! Hey, since the adults are the ones who pay the tithe in the church and keep the building running so you've got a warm place to meet, would you mind giving us some of those snacks for our class? We've only got ten people—we shouldn't need more than about half the food." Tell the youth it's up to them and wait for their reaction. After the adult volunteer has left

(with or without food!), sound the youth out about how they felt when such a request was made. Let them know that today's story is about a person who was having a party and had a similar request made of him.

OPTION B

Welcome the youth to the classroom and spend a few minutes checking in on their lives since your last session. After a bit of conversation, ask the youth if they've ever had to smooth something over with someone. Was there an impending argument that they had to avert? Specifically, ask if they ever had to intervene on someone else's behalf, such as between a friend of theirs and a teacher. What did they do? What were the results?

Let them know that today's story is about a woman who had to avert a potentially deadly dispute between her husband and a stranger.

Telling the Story
(5–10 minutes)
OPTION A

Needed: costumes and props (optional), Bibles

This is a great story for acting out, so allow your youth to really get into it. You may choose to assign parts (David, Abigail, Nabal, David's messenger, Nabal's servant, David's army, other partygoers, etc.) as you have youth, making sure that everyone has some part. The actors may then mime the story as a narrator reads it, or you might have them read their lines out of the Bible, with you acting as narrator. Another option would be to divide the story into parts and assign each part of the story to smaller groups, who would then act out their part for the rest of the class. Some natural divisions of 1 Samuel 25 would be the following:

Scene 1: We meet the main characters; David sends his request to Nabal (vv. 1-8).

Scene 2: Nabal makes his response to the messenger (vv. 9-11).

Scene 3: The messenger returns to David with Nabal's response (vv. 12-13).

Scene 4: Abigail hears of the exchange from another servant (vv. 14-19).

Scene 5: Abigail and David meet; Abigail makes her supplication (vv. 20-35).

Scene 6: Abigail tells Nabal about the events the next day (vv. 36-38).

Scene 7: Nabal dies; David and Abigail marry (vv. 39-44).

Make such costumes and props available as you may have access to.

OPTION B

Needed: Bibles

This story contains many characters. The three main ones, of course, are Abigail, David, and Nabal, but there are many others (see the listing in Option A). Invite the class members to each choose a particular character—one of the three main ones or someone less specific, such as a member of the army or a party guest. As you read the story together, encourage the youth to view the story from the perspective of their particular character. They are to imagine what that character might have seen, heard, felt, and thought about the events of the story. Read the story together in whatever form your class prefers.

Reacting to the Story (10–15 minutes)

OPTION A

Needed: Bibles, newsprint and markers (optional)

Invite the youth to share any questions or comments they have about the story. Are there any parts of the story that seem odd to them? Uncomfortable? Do they agree or disagree with the actions of the characters in the story? What do they think about David and Abigail getting married at the end? What do they think about Nabal's fate?

As questions or comments are raised, continually refer the youth back to the story itself; encourage them to scan the story again. Can they find clues to their questions in the text or not? Consider taking notes about their responses on newsprint, especially any questions that are raised, for reference later.

OPTION B

(This option is most effective if it follows Option B of "Telling the Story.")

Needed: Bibles

For this step, the youth will be sharing their reactions to having read the story from the perspective of one of its characters. Remind them to keep in mind the character they chose from "Telling the Story" during this step. If you've got a larger class, break the youth into small groups, making sure each small group has a good mix of characters from the story. Invite the youth to spend a few minutes sharing what they think their character might have been experiencing in the story.

Consider asking them to stay in character and share their reactions using "I" statements. This will be particularly interesting if they can have conversations with the other characters in the story, such as one of the party guests talking with one of the members of David's army.

They can imagine as much as they choose, but they need to stay true to the story itself. What might one of Nabal's servants have to say to Nabal himself—for example, about Nabal's response to David? Allow them several minutes for their sharing together.

If you have time, or possibly instead of mixing the characters, consider having the youth gather with other youth who chose the same character they did. As a group, invite them to come up with a character sketch of the person they chose, describing the person as clearly as they can, including how the person might have looked, dressed, talked, and walked and what his or her personality might have been like. After they've done so, they should share their group character sketch with the rest of the class.

Connecting to the Story (10–15 minutes)
OPTION A
Needed: newsprint and markers or chalkboard and chalk (optional)
Invite the class to spend a moment or two brainstorming names of music groups, local organizations, and so forth, considering names that have some meaning. For example, the Christian alternative group Jars of Clay chose their name to point out a particular aspect of their belief. What are some of the class members' favorite music groups (Christian

or secular)? Do the groups' names mean anything? For local organizations, how might the name be important? Consider Habitat for Humanity, for example. What does the name say about the organization and its goals? (Encourage the youth to go beyond the obvious.) Are there any geographic names that have meaning? Do they know why your town or city is named what it is?

Explain to the class that names in the Bible often have significance and should be paid attention to when we're interpreting a story. Point out to the class verse 25 of the story, in which Abigail makes a play on words using Nabal's name. Invite them to consider biblical names that have meaning from stories they've heard before. As they share their responses, consider writing the responses on chalkboard or newsprint. (If the class is new to the Bible, skip this step.) Follow this with Option A of "Exploring the Story."

OPTION B
Needed: Bibles, commentaries
Break the class into two groups: a "David" group and a "Nabal" group. Make sure each group has adequate access to Bibles and commentaries. Have the groups study the events of the story from their assigned character's point of view, trying to be as sympathetic to their character as possible. For example, what good reasons might David have had to react to Nabal's response the way he did? What good reasons might Nabal have had to be cautious about David's request? Your youth might need to use their imaginations on this, and

the commentaries can be of help in understanding the historical and cultural situation of the time.

After they've had a few minutes to come up with their sympathetic viewpoints, have the two groups enter into a conversation with each other as if they were their characters. This is not a debate so much as an organized sharing of viewpoints.

Exploring the Story
(10–15 minutes)
OPTION A
Needed: "What's in a Name?" handouts, writing utensils, Bibles, name definition books (such as baby name books), Bible study aids
Give a copy of the "What's in a Name?" handout and a writing utensil to each person. Invite them to complete only Part I at this time. Make sure they have adequate access to Bibles, name definition books, and other Bible study helps as listed above. Give them several minutes to work on their handouts. If you think they'd be more comfortable doing so, they may work in pairs or triads. After they've had some time, bring the class back together to share their responses to Part I.

Then, after their sharing, consider the lists of names you discussed in Option A of "Connecting to the Story." Would any of the names of musical groups or organizations fit into the biblical concept of the importance of naming? Why or why not? What kind of power seems to be given to names in the Bible? (In other words, is there power involved in the ability to give a name or in knowing someone's name?) Compare this with today: is there any "power" involved in giv-

ing a name or knowing a name? (For example, parents giving a child a name, or the relatively recent habit of strangers using your first name on first acquaintance.)

OPTION B
Needed: "Exploration Points" handouts, writing utensils, study Bibles, Bible study aids, including commentaries on 1 Samuel
Give a copy of the "Exploration Points" handout and a writing utensil to each youth. Make sure there are adequate Bible study helps available. Invite them to read over the four Exploration Points listed on the handout and choose one that particularly interests them for further study. Some of the points need the study helps; others could be accomplished using only Bibles (although even these would benefit from other helps being available). If you choose, you may have the class form into smaller study groups based on the Exploration Points chosen—all who choose Point A working together, etc.

After the class members have had adequate time for their study, bring them back together to share their findings.

Then, after they've shared, invite them to consider what difference this new knowledge makes to their understanding of 1 Samuel 25, if any.

Living the Story
(5–10 minutes)
OPTION A
(This option follows Option A of "Exploring the Story.")
Needed: "What's in a Name?" handouts, writing utensils, baby name books

Invite class members to spend a few moments completing Part II of the "What's in a Name?" handout. After they've done so, get them into pairs or triads to share their "name stories" and responses to the other questions in Part II. Bring them back together and lead a discussion using questions like the following:

■ Do you have any other "names," such as names in a different language or nicknames? If so, what do these names mean?

■ Does your church have special naming traditions (christenings, baptism names, etc.)?

Once you've discussed some of these things, read together Acts 3:1-8,16 and Ephesians 3:14-15. Discuss: *What does it mean to do something in the name of Christ? To take your name from God?* Suggest to the youth that to bear the name Christian implies certain things. Have them brainstorm what these might be. Is that a name they feel prepared to live up to?

OPTION B
Needed: candle, matches or lighter, quiet background music on CD, CD player
Have the youth read 1 Samuel 24 and 1 Samuel 26, first giving them the background information that Saul was the king who became threatened by David's obvious personal charisma and power and sought to kill David before David became a threat to Saul's throne. In these two stories David seems to be handed golden opportunities to rid himself of Saul forever.

After the youth have had an opportunity to skim the stories, discuss the stories in chapters 24–26:

■ What made David want revenge in each of these stories?

■ What happened to keep him from exacting his revenge?

■ What did David learn about revenge from these stories?

■ What effect might these experiences have had on him later on, when he was king?

■ What does God seem to think about the human habit of wanting revenge? (For example, what do you think God would have to say about the old bumper sticker that said, "I don't get mad, I get even"?)

Light the candle and play the quiet background music, inviting the youth to get comfortable. Lead them in a time of prayer, asking them to offer up to God their own desires for revenge or for getting even. Be sure to allow some time for silent reflection as a part of their prayer time.

Things to Ponder
Some youth have grown up in families whose relationships often seem based on revenge and getting even. For these youth, some of today's discussion topics might be difficult to grasp or even uncomfortable. As always, follow up where you feel appropriate, and pray for the youth by name both before and after the class, during your own personal prayer time.

Looking Ahead
Depending on which options you choose, you may need to find a copy of the Disney movie *Pinnochio* and have it cued to the appropriate place (see the next session for more specifics). You may also need to find a CD of whale songs.

What's in a Name?

Part I

In the Bible, we often get clues to the story by looking at the meaning of a person's name. Read the following Scriptures and fill in the chart below. You might need to use the Bible study helps available to look up the names. You may not be able to fill in each part for every character, but do the best you can!

Scripture	Person's Name	Meaning of Name	What "clue" to the story does the name give you?
Genesis 3:20			
Genesis 17:3-5			
Genesis 17:15-16			
Genesis 32:24-28			
Isaiah 7:14			
Matthew 1:20-21			
Matthew 16:17-19			

Part II

What does your name mean? Look your name up in the name definition book. (If your name isn't in there, find the closest form of it, or look up a middle name.) Write the definition here:

Do you think that definition fits you or your life story? Why or why not?

Does your name seem to express certain expectations about your life? What are those expectations? Do you think you can live up to them? (If your name doesn't have a particular meaning but has a family story behind it, consider that story for this question.)

~~~~~~

Exploration Points

Choose one of the following subjects to explore further, and see how it might help in your interpretation of today's Scripture story.

Point A: Naming in the Bible

Look up "name" in a Bible dictionary and see what importance names had in biblical times. List two or three times when names and their definitions are given in Bible stories (for example, Abram's name being changed to Abraham in Genesis 17:3-5). Do names give some sort of clues to the person who is given that name, or to their life story, in the Bible? Do you think they still do today? Why or why not?

Point B: David's Band of Followers

Nabal might have had good reason to be a little nervous about David, although he had equally good reason to be grateful to David. Read the following passages, and use the back of this page to list everything you can find out about David's army. Who was in it? How many? What did they do? Do they remind you of any other famous groups of people, either in the Bible or in literature through the ages? How so?

Scriptures to read: 1 Samuel 22:1-2; 23:1-5; 25:5-8,14-16 (excerpts from today's story)

Point C: Sheepshearing Festival

Obviously, there was a reason why David decided to send his request to Nabal during Nabal's sheepshearing. You will need to use Bible encyclopedias or dictionaries for this step. Spend a few minutes exploring sheepshearing and related festivals in biblical times. After you know a little more about them, figure out why it might have been good for David to wait until just this time to contact Nabal with his request for provisions for his army.

Point D: Marriage in Old Testament Times

To us, it might seem a little odd, if not downright distasteful, for Abigail to be rushing off to marry David so soon after her husband died, and after meeting David only once for a few minutes. Besides that, she was not his only wife! People had a different understanding of marriage in Old Testament times, and that might help us to better understand how this could be considered a "happy ending." Using Bible encyclopedias, dictionaries, and commentaries on this passage, explore what marriage meant to the man and to the woman. Consider, also, why it might have been significant to David to marry a Calebite woman during his rise to power.

13. Jonah

Bible Story: Jonah

Wallace Smith

A Story behind the Story

When we approach the theological theme of salvation, most likely we immediately think of Jesus and the stories of Jesus' death and resurrection in the Gospels and Epistles of the New Testament. Yet God's saving power is evident well beyond our focus in the New Testament, and the thread of salvation runs throughout the story of God recorded in the Bible!

This session focuses upon Jonah, the reluctant prophet. Set in the middle of the Book of the Twelve Prophets (otherwise known as the Minor Prophets), the story of Jonah is unique among these books. Instead of being filled with eloquent and prophetic messages from the prophet himself, the Book of Jonah is a story about one man's response to God's call, his personal struggle, and the amazing way God can work through us all, in spite of ourselves.

God called Jonah to preach to the people of Nineveh, the capital of the Assyrian Empire, which was a sworn enemy and oppressor of the Israelites. Jonah was a person who was reluctant and perhaps selfish and stubborn, who wanted nothing to do with his enemies and certainly did not want to preach about the God of Israel in the center of the "evil empire." We are, of course, familiar with the "fish story" found in the middle of Jonah's story, but we're perhaps less familiar with the whole story of Jonah's repentance, in which he finally did what God called him to do, then became upset when the outcome was not what he wanted. God showed mercy, the Ninevites were saved, and Jonah was a grudging witness to God's salvation.

Yet there are still other layers to this story of salvation. On Jonah's journey in the opposite direction of Nineveh, toward Tarshish, he inadvertently shared the message and power of God with superstitious sailors, who turned to God and were saved. Jonah himself was "saved" by the fish that God sent, and so he was given a second chance. There are even more threads of God's salvation woven throughout the fabric of this familiar story. This lesson is an opportunity to explore and find those threads that we may have passed over before. Enjoy the journey with Jonah!

Enter the Story

Take time during the week before presenting this lesson to read and reflect on the story of Jonah several times. You may want to read the story at the beginning and ending of each day, so that the story becomes very familiar.

As the story is fresh in your mind, at times during the day you may find yourself reflecting on the story of Jonah as that story intersects with your own story. Where in your life story have you felt like Jonah? When have you acted like Jonah? Are there places, people, or situations in your life that are like Nineveh for you? You may find it helpful to record your thoughts in a journal as you prepare to share this learning experience with your group.

POSSIBLE YOUTH CONTACT POINTS

- Is God calling me in some way?
- What does God expect of me?
- What do I expect of God?
- What do I struggle with in faith?
- What or whom do I avoid?
- Do I always insist on my way?

YOU MAY NEED

- tent or sheets and blankets
- TV and VCR
- video of Disney's *Pinocchio*
- Bibles
- flashlights
- CD of whale songs (preferably without music accompaniment)
- CD player
- newsprint
- markers
- tape
- paper
- writing utensils
- "Jonah's Journey/My Journey" handouts
- "Something Far Greater than Jonah" handouts
- Bible study aids, such as encyclopedias, commentaries, maps
- candle
- matches or lighter
- ball of yarn or string
- CD of soft background music

Setting the Stage (5–10 minutes)

OPTION A

Needed: tent or sheets and blankets to make a "cave"

Take time to set up your meeting space with a dark environment to tell the story. You could use a tent or blankets over tables and chairs to make a cavelike "dark belly of the fish." As the youth enter the room, use a blanket to "swallow them up" one at a time and place them in the belly of the fish. The youth may feel unsure about sharing such close quarters, so explain to them that you hope the experience will help them hear a familiar story in a new way.

Once everyone has arrived and is well situated in "the belly," discuss the following questions. (Feel free to have fun with the first few; the remainder become gradually more serious.)

- Does anyone have a good "fish story" to tell?
- What do you think it would be like to be inside a fish for three days?
- Tell about a time when you felt compelled or "called" to do something. Did you do it? Why or why not?
- Tell about a time when your life felt like a storm.
- Tell about a time when you felt furthest from God.

After the discussion, move on to telling the story of Jonah. (Option A of "Telling the Story" most suitably follows this option. However, either option may be used successfully.)

OPTION B

Needed: video of Disney's **Pinocchio**, *TV and VCR*

Before the session, you will need to cue the video to the scene in which Geppetto's boat is in the storm and then is swallowed by the whale. As youth enter the room, have the video playing in the background. Ask the participants, *Do you know what book of the Bible we will read today?* and see if they can guess the story. If they do so and seem to have some previous knowledge of the story of Jonah, feel free to take a few moments to discuss similarities and differences between Jonah's story and that of Pinocchio, just for fun. While the Pinocchio story is not the story of Jonah, the images of the cartoon may create a more vivid picture of Jonah when you tell the story later on.

Telling the Story (5–10 minutes)

OPTION A

(This option best follows Option A of "Setting the Stage.")

Needed: Bibles, flashlights (if you are inside your "fish belly"), whale songs CD and CD player

Make sure every participant has a Bible or shares a Bible so that everyone can read and follow along. Ask the youth to find the Book of Jonah in their Bibles. As some individuals may not be comfortable reading in front of the large group, ask for volunteers to read the story out loud. You will need at least four volunteers to tell the story, each reading a chapter of Jonah for the group. You can, of course, use as many volunteers to read the story as you want, dividing the Scripture into sections, figuring out ahead of time the distinct characters' voices and assigning these parts, or simply reading the story "popcorn" style around the group. What is important is that everyone can see the Scripture while it is read out loud.

Consider playing a CD of whale songs (preferably one without music accompaniment, if you can find it) during the reading. For greater effect, have the CD placed outside of the tent "fish belly," then excuse yourself from the group briefly to turn it on and return, so that the youth are not expecting the sounds during the reading.

OPTION B

Needed: Bibles, newsprint, markers, tape

The story of Jonah lends itself to being told in a visual way. Divide the larger group into four teams. Give each team a chapter of Jonah to read as a group. Tell the groups to read their chapter out loud together, and then work as a group to make a cartoon version of the story. As a group, they will need to create a series or panels of pictures (stick figures are just fine) that tell the story of their chapter. Encourage them to have fun with the pictures, but remind them not to add or reword any part of the Scripture—their job is simply to tell the story of their chapter using pictures.

Have each group tell the story from their chapter to the larger group using their cartoon panels. Then tape the panels to the wall in proper sequence.

Reacting to the Story (15–20 minutes)

OPTION A

Needed: Bibles, newsprint, markers

Ask the participants to form groups of three and answer the following questions together:

■ What did you hear in this story that you have never noticed before?
■ What was funny about this story?

■ What questions do you have about the story?

After participants have had an opportunity to react and share their impressions, ask them to discuss these questions:

■ Why do you think Jonah did not want to go to Nineveh?
■ What is Jonah upset about?
■ How and why was the wicked city of Nineveh saved?
■ How was Jonah saved?
■ Was Jonah saved more than once in the story?
■ Did Jonah understand that he had been saved?

Once the small groups have had an opportunity to discuss their responses to the questions, have them create a brief dramatic representation of their thoughts for the rest of the class. They might have one person act the part of Jonah while a second person interviews him as for an evening news broadcast. The third person might be one of the sailors or a Ninevite, interviewed for an opposing point of view. Another option might be to have Jonah as an old man talking with his two great-grandchildren, telling the story again from the perspective of years having passed. Or the group might want to rewrite the story in modern-day terms. The triads may do whatever they choose—just remind them of how much time they have to plan and rehearse, and allow time for the triads to present.

OPTION B

Needed: Bibles, paper, writing utensils

Share with the youth that, when we hear the familiar story of Jonah, many times we remember the part about Jonah and the great fish but we lose sight of the rest of the characters and the meaning of the story. Ask the participants:

- How would you identify with each of the characters of the story?
- What do you think is important about the different characters in the story?

Have the participants make a list on paper of the characters in the story, including God, Jonah, the sailors, the great fish, the king, the Ninevites, the plant, and the worm. Have them write a sentence next to each character about that character's role in the story. Or have them write what they think the message of the story is from the perspective of each character.

Connecting the Story (15–20 minutes)
OPTION A
Needed: "Jonah's Journey/My Journey" handouts, writing utensils
As you distribute copies of the handout, tell the participants that they will be making a map of their own life journey in comparison to Jonah's. Some of the youth may not be comfortable or able to make a "faith journey" map, but they could easily make highlights of their life and life choices that may include faith events, a sense of "calling," or times when they turned away from something, only later to reverse a decision and get back on a previous life path. Ask the youth:

- Have you ever felt or acted like Jonah?
- Is there a place or a time that has been "Nineveh" for you?
- Are there times in your life that you remember making choices that seemed to greatly impact your life journey?

Then give them time to make their own life journey on the activity sheet.

OPTION B
Needed: Bibles, paper, writing utensils
If you have more than ten people in your class, divide them into two groups so that everyone can have time to share. Otherwise, with the class together as a whole, ask the participants to share any personal connection or learning they have with the story of Jonah. Discuss:

- Has there been a time when you have felt you should say something to a group of people to change their behavior but you just weren't sure if you should or could do it?
- What did you do?
- How did you feel?
- What happened as a result?

This may also be a time to discuss individuals' connections with Jonah's feelings of anger at God.

In Jonah's prayer to God (2:1-9) he offered words of lament and a promise that are similar to those of some other psalms and lamentations in the Bible. Jonah thanked God for saving him and made a new vow to be faithful to God. Reread Jonah's prayer as a group, then give each participant time to think about his or her own life, times of struggle, and commitment to God. Invite participants to write their own psalm or prayer to God, using some psalms as reference (for example, Psalms 13, 16, 30, and 56).

Exploring the Story (15–20 minutes)
OPTION A
Needed: Bibles, Bible study aids, newsprint and markers

Invite the youth to dig deeper into the story by reading related Scriptures, to understand Jonah's reaction to God's call, Jonah's reasons for not wanting to go to Nineveh, and Jonah's anger for God's mercy for the Ninevites. Have written on newsprint ahead of time some chapters for them to consider: 2 Kings 24–25, Isaiah 10, Nahum 2–3, Joel 2. You might also find other Scriptures listed in your Bible if you have a Bible with study notes or Scripture references.

Encourage the youth to use various biblical and interpretive tools (Bible encyclopedias and commentaries) to learn about Israel in the time of Jonah, Israel's enemies the Assyrians, and the city of Nineveh. Study maps of the Old Testament, and map Jonah's physical journey from the beginning, on the boat to Tarshish, and eventually to Nineveh. Divide the various interpretive resources around the group, give time for research, and then discuss your findings. If you have a larger group or less time, have the class break into smaller groups of three to four people, and assign each one of the above listed aspects to study.

When all of the groups have done their work, have them share their findings with the class as a whole. Once that is done, be sure to have the youth reconsider the Scripture in light of their research: Do any of their findings change previous notions about the meaning of Scripture? Do they have a better understanding of Jonah's reluctance? Do they have a better feel for the situation at Nineveh?

OPTION B
Needed: Bibles, "Something Far Greater than Jonah" handouts, writing utensils
In the story of Jonah, there is "something far greater than Jonah" that is taking place, for God was at work in spite of Jonah. Through Jonah's message, the people of Nineveh repented and were saved. Jesus, when confronted by Israelites who demanded proof of who he was, referred to the sign of Jonah and the faithfulness of the Ninevites (Matthew 12:38-41; Luke 11:29-32). Invite the youth to use the activity sheet "Something Far Greater than Jonah" to compare Jonah's journey and message to Jesus' journey and message, and to explore the ways God is present.

Living the Story (5-10 minutes)
OPTION A
Needed: candle, matches or lighter, ball of yarn or string, CD player and CD of soft background music (optional)
Gather the group in a circle. Light the candle and encourage the youth to focus on the flame. In your own words, say something like this:
This ball of string represents your connection to the story and the connection among members in the group as you have shared the story. Threads of God's salvation are woven through the story of Jonah. These connections or threads have revealed a picture of God's mercy, God's justice, and God's will. In a brief word or phrase, as we go around the circle, share a connection you have had with the story.

Pass the ball of string around the circle and affirm each person as he or she shares. When one person passes the ball to the next person, that person should be sure to hang on to one part of the string so that the string forms a circle connecting each person to the whole group. When the string makes it around the circle, close your time together with prayer for God's guidance with the places or people in life that are like Nineveh for us, and for our understanding of God's grace and God's will in our own lives.

OPTION B
Needed: "Jonah's Journey/My Journey" handouts or written psalms from "Connecting to the Story"
Have the youth bring their life maps or their psalms (from "Connecting to the Story") to the closing circle and invite each person to share one thing from her or his "connection." Consider allowing youth the option to "pass" on the sharing if they feel their work is far too personal or if the group has not been together long enough to have built a strong foundation of trust. For the faith journey map, it may be the direction they are currently heading toward or a future "destination." For the psalm, it may be the commitment they have written at the end of their prayer.

After each person has shared (or has chosen to pass), ask:
■ How do you think God's justice was shown in the story?
■ Are justice and mercy the same thing?

■ Do you see God's justice and mercy in your life map or psalm?
Close with a prayer for God's guidance and strength when the journey is not easy.

Things to Ponder
The story of Jonah reads like a comedy-tragedy. There are funny elements to the story. Our image of Jonah is usually similar to that of Zacchaeus or George Costanza from *Seinfeld*—a small, unsure man. But there is also a sadness for the bumbling and stubborn Jonah. Does Jonah ever "get it" in the end when God teaches him how deeply God cares about all living things, even our enemies?

This is an easy story to relate to, because Jonah is an easy person for us to relate to: he is stubborn, he is selfish, he questions God, he wants his own way—he's human, just like us! Be aware that under the comedy of the story are deep questions of faith and life with which youth will identify. Youth may be very observant of Jonah's shortcomings, but they may not openly identify them with their own image issues and faith questions.

Looking Ahead
Depending on which option you choose, you may need to seek out an adult volunteer (an "elder" person) who would be willing and able to come to your class to talk about her or his faith story.

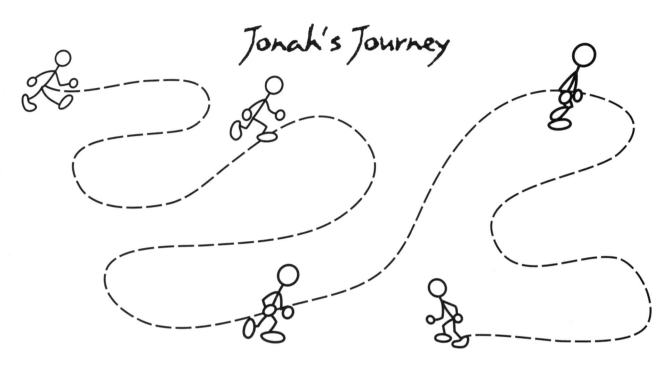

Jonah's Journey

My Journey

Something Far Greater than Jonah

Read the story of Jesus speaking about Jonah
(Matthew 12:38-41 or Luke 11:29-32).

1. To whom was Jesus talking?

2. What was Jesus saying about Jonah and the Ninevites?

3. What was Jesus saying about himself?

In the two columns below, compare Jonah and Jesus.

Jonah's Journey (Jonah 1:1-3,17; 3:1-3)	**Jesus' Journey** (Matthew 16:21-28; Luke 9:22-27)
Jonah's Message (Jonah 3:4)	**Jesus' Message** (Matthew 22:34-40; Matthew 25:31-46; Luke 10:25-28)
The Result (Jonah 3:5-10; 4)	**The Result?**

What do the Book of Jonah and the life, ministry, and death of Jesus teach about God's salvation?

What is the "something far greater than Jonah" that Jesus offers his followers?

14. Simeon and Anna

Bible Story: Luke 2:25-38

Wallace Smith

A Story behind the Story

The Book of Luke is the only one of the four Gospels that gives us any stories of Jesus as a child. Luke shows us the connections between Jesus and the prophecies of the Old Testament. It shows us as well the promise of the Messiah who would redeem Israel. In Simeon and Anna, we find a representation of the Israel that is faithful to God: they were devout, wise, prayerful, led by the Spirit, and looking with hope toward tomorrow for the fulfillment of God's promise of the Messiah.

We enjoy telling and hearing the stories of the Light of the World entering in, but we must remember that light has darkness flitting around the edges—with Jesus' coming, we are brought to the point of decision. Old ways are turned on their head, the comfortable are made to feel discomfited, the last are first, and the highest are lowered. Jesus would not have an easy life; nor would his mother be able to watch his growing up from a cozy position in a rocking chair. Simeon offered the warning: the soul-piercing sword would strike (Luke 2:35).

We sympathize with the mother just as we feel our own nervousness. What does Christ's coming mean to us? Should not our own souls be pierced? Not, of course, with the pain of a mother watching her son dying on a cross, but with the pain of one who is made to reflect upon his or her own life and see its lack. Are we being disciples as we should be? Do we live up to the name of Christian?

And yet the hope is still there—the hope that justice may come and that God's will may truly be done on earth. The joy is still there—the joy that God loves us to this extent, beyond life itself. The promise is believed: what God began in creation is continued, culminated, in the birth of a child.

In the story of Simeon and Anna in the temple with the baby Jesus, we have a beautiful and powerful image of prophecy fulfilled. Fragile hands, wrinkled and spotted with age, hold up with renewed strength a delicate baby. Weathered and teary eyes behold with joy the face of the baby Jesus, realizing the fulfillment of a lifetime of faith and waiting in hope. Immanuel: God is with us! And Anna immediately begins to tell the story to all who are gathered in the temple courtyard: the Messiah has finally come!

Enter the Story

Take time to read the story reflectively. Pay special attention to Simeon and Anna, and think of a time in your life when you waited a long time for something. Also, be aware of the mix of emotions that Mary and Joseph must have felt as new parents, with strangers approaching their baby, and then hearing the words of prophecy from these older people! What do the words "and a sword shall pierce your soul, as well" mean?

POSSIBLE YOUTH CONTACT POINTS

- How can I possibly be compared to Jesus?
- What do my parents expect of me?
- What are some dreams and possibilities for my life?
- What am I looking forward to?
- What will life be like when I am older?
- How does God measure faithfulness?
- How can I share my faith in Jesus?

YOU MAY NEED

- "Birth Announcement" handouts
- ink pads
- markers
- Bibles, a variety of translations, including a contemporary translation such as *The Message*
- newsprint
- "Encounter with the Baby Jesus" handouts
- a special guest who is an elder in your church or grandparent figure for the youth
- paper
- writing utensils
- Bible study aids, such as Bible encyclopedias, dictionaries, commentaries, etc.
- candle
- matches or lighter
- ball of yarn or string

Take time to pray for each person who may be participating in this session, especially for their connections to the story as they encounter Simeon and Anna and the Light to the Nations!

Setting the Stage (5–10 minutes)

OPTION A

Needed: "Birth Announcement" handouts, ink pads, markers

Have each participant make his or her "birth announcement" on the activity page. Explain the process to the youth. Using the ink pad, they should make a fist and press the bottom side (the "pinkie" side) of the fist into the ink and then make an impression on the page to make each "foot." Then they can use their fingerprints in the ink pad to make "toes." Have them fill in the certificate by writing their name and birthday, but leave the lines on the bottom left-hand corner blank. Remind the youth to leave room, because participants will add to their birth announcement during "Connecting to the Story."

As a group, make a list of the ways we recognize and celebrate babies and birth. (For example: "Our family put a sign in the yard and sent out announcements for my little sister" or "Our church puts a rose on the pulpit each time a baby is born into a congregation family.") Finally, tell the group that today you are going to explore a story about the baby Jesus and his parents following the Jewish customs for infants. This leads to an encounter in the temple courtyard with Simeon and Anna.

OPTION B

For this step, you will be playing "Simeon Says." (You'd be surprised how many youth love to play childhood games! We often worry that they might think it's too silly, but most youth appreciate an opportunity to act childish—with permission!—again.) Tell your class that Simeon was a wise and righteous man in Israel, a respected elder of the community, and a teacher in the temple. Explain: *Today our classroom is the temple, and since I am the oldest and wisest person in the room, I will be Simeon. Let's play "Simeon Says"!* Play a round or two of "Simon Says" with the group, substituting "Simon" with "Simeon." Make up your own instructions for the game, but also throw in some related to the story, such as "Simeon says say a prayer" or "Simeon says praise God" or "Simeon says comfort your neighbor."

Telling the Story (5–10 minutes)

OPTION A

Needed: Bibles

Ask for four volunteers from the group. Assign each volunteer a part: Simeon, Mary, Joseph, and Anna. Give them a moment to quickly read the Scripture and then have them "mime" the Scripture while you read it out loud for the larger group. It may be fun to have the volunteers simply react to the story as you read it, but if the actors struggle, here are a few hints:

- Simeon—Act old and wise, gesture with your hands as you "tell" about the great things ahead for the baby Jesus, gently console Mary as "a sword shall pierce your soul too" is spoken.

116

- Mary and Joseph—Act amazed at what is being said about your baby, even though you have previously been visited by angels, shepherds, and wise men!
- Anna—Your actions may be directed to the audience, as they are in the "temple," and you can spread the word about the Messiah to them.

If the youth really enjoy themselves and others would like to volunteer, feel free to do the mime again with a different set of volunteers.

OPTION B
Needed: different translations of the Bible, including **The Message** *or another contemporary version*
Ask for volunteers to read the story "in the round." You may want to read from a variety of translations of the Bible, reading verse by verse around the group until the story is finished. If you use *The Message,* you may want to finish by reading the story in its entirety, as this contemporary version only references verse numbers at the top of each page. After the youth have heard the story, invite discussion about the different versions (particularly if using *The Message*). Ask:
- Did the different wordings confuse you?
- Were there any parts that seemed more clear when hearing them from a different version? Why is that?
- What is the benefit to reading a story in a different version on occasion?

Reacting to the Story (15–20 minutes)
OPTION A
Needed: Bibles, "Encounter with the Baby Jesus" handouts, writing utensils, paper (optional)

Using the activity handout, ask participants to write responses to the story from the perspective of the characters in the story. The handout helps the youth respond to such questions as these:
- What was Simeon feeling when he first saw the baby Jesus?
- What was Mary's reaction to these words from strangers in the temple courtyard?
- How did Joseph respond to this attention given to his son?
- How did Anna know who Jesus was?

After they've finished working on the handout, invite the youth to share their responses as they may be comfortable doing so, perhaps using the questions above to spark further conversation.

If you have enough time, and if your group enjoys creative exercises, invite each youth to choose one character in the story with whom he or she identifies and write the story as if being told by that character to his or her grandchildren years later (or in the case of the elderly Simeon and Anna, as if they were telling it to their neighbors a few years later). Encourage the youth to include as many details as possible to make the story come alive for them. (They may use the back of the handout to do their writing, or you may want to provide writing paper.)

OPTION B
Needed: Bibles, newsprint, markers
Have the group create a list on newsprint of the emotions and images that come to mind when they hear the story. They may choose to use one-word responses or phrases.

After you have a good list, discuss these questions and record their responses also on newsprint (either the same sheet or a different one if you don't have enough room):

- What do you imagine the temple to be like?
- What do Simeon and Anna look like?
- What emotions do Simeon and Anna have when they encounter Jesus?
- What do Joseph and Mary feel?

Ask the group if they have any questions regarding the story. Make a list of the questions and save them to use as a part of "Exploring the Story."

Connecting to the Story (15–20 minutes)

OPTION A

Needed: a special guest

If you can arrange it before the session, invite an elder in your church to come to the session and share a story of faith—a time in his or her life when this person had great expectations for an event and had to have patience and faith while awaiting the outcome. Ask the visitor to read the Scripture ahead of time and share with the group any connections this person has to the story from his or her perspective and life experiences. Once the visitor has shared, thank this elder for participating and allow him or her to leave.

After the visitor has left, ask the youth to discuss:

- What could you learn from this person's story?
- Would you consider this person a "Simeon" or an "Anna"?

- What questions of faith and life may this person be able to answer?
- What can you gain from listening to a grandparent figure or one of the "pillars" of your church as such a person reflects on his or her hopes and dreams and prayers of faith?

OPTION B

(This option should follow Option A of "Setting the Stage.")

Needed: "Birth Announcement" handouts, writing utensils

Ask the group to close their eyes and picture a newborn baby. Invite the group to silently reflect on the following questions. (Read them with pauses in between so the youth can focus on each question.)

- What are the baby's needs?
- What do we expect of the parents?
- What are the promises and possibilities of this new life and the future years that this baby looks forward to?

Allow the youth to open their eyes. Tell the group in your own words that many prophecies and expectations about Jesus were shared with Joseph and Mary by angels as well as by Simeon and Anna as they celebrated the life of this fragile baby in the temple. Joseph and Mary had expectations for their son, yet there were even larger promises and expectations that came from those who awaited the coming of the Messiah. Ask: *What do you think the promises and possibilities were for you when you were a newborn baby, and what do you think your future holds?*

Directing the youth to their birth announcements from earlier, have them list and celebrate the possibilities and dreams they have for their lives in the section "Celebration of Life." Some of those promises and expectations may already be fulfilled; some dreams may be for the not-yet-known future.

Exploring the Story (15–20 minutes)
OPTION A
Needed: Bibles, Bible encyclopedias, writing utensils, paper
This is a story that connects us with the traditions of Jesus' time and the context of the Jewish faith. Invite the youth to take this opportunity to investigate and explore the answers to the questions they raised in Option B of "Reacting to the Story," if you chose that option.

Alternatively, they might explore one of the following subjects related to Jewish life: customs and traditions related to newborn infants, the role of the temple, or the rite of circumcision. Other subjects to explore include any Scripture notes and connections of Simeon's words to Joseph and Mary, along with the role of prophecy and prophets in biblical times. If you've got a larger class, or if you feel it might be more effective, have the youth get into pairs or triads and choose one topic to study as a group.

After they've had some time to gather information, invite the youth (either as individuals or small groups) to share their findings with the class as a whole. Take a few moments, after they've all shared, to discuss what effect, if any, this new information has on their understanding of the Scripture story.

OPTION B
Needed: Bibles, Bible study aids, writing utensils, paper
Invite the youth to explore Bible connections and expectations regarding the Messiah. Consider writing the following questions ahead of time on newsprint, breaking the class into pairs or triads to use the resources in order to shape their responses to the following questions:
■ What is said about the baby Jesus as the Messiah in the story?
■ What do these other Scripture connections in the Gospels say about the Messiah: Matthew 1:17-23 and Luke 19:9-10?
■ Use another resource (Bible encyclopedia, commentary, etc.) and find something out about the Messiah from that resource.
■ What does the Old Testament say about the Messiah (some passages to consider: Isaiah 42:6; 49:6; 52:10; 59:21; 61:1-11)?
■ A Christian perspective can be found in Romans 4:21-25. What other Scriptures can you find that tell who Jesus is as the Messiah (or the Christ)?
■ What did you learn about the Messiah or the prophecies of salvation that you did not realize before?

Living the Story (5–10 minutes)
OPTION A
(This option should follow Option B of "Connecting to the Story.")
Needed: "Birth Announcement" handouts
Gather in a circle and thank the group for their work during the session. Take a few moments to review some of the highlights of

the session—activities you did together, some of the discussions, and so on. Ask the youth questions like the following to help them review their experience of the story:

■ What was the most surprising thing you discovered about the Scripture during the session?

■ Do you think differently about the story now than you did when you first heard it? If so, what's the difference? If not, why not?

■ What is your favorite part of the story?

After the discussion, invite the group to share their birth announcement and the dreams and possibilities they wrote. Suggest, after the sharing, that they keep these birth announcements at home, someplace where they might see it often or find it again at important junctures of their lives (birthdays, for example, or the first day of a new school year). Offer affirmations to each participant and close the session with a prayer for the possibilities shared and for God's light on the journey ahead.

OPTION B

Needed: candle, matches or lighter, ball of string

Light the candle and gather around the candle in a circle. As the youth focus on the light of the candle, ask them in your own words to reflect on the connections or "threads" of God's justice and mercy that were woven throughout the story. Today's session had themes of expectation and waiting in faith, waiting for God's promise of salvation, the promise of liberation to the people of Israel.

As you pass the ball of string around, ask each person to share a word or phrase representing a connection they made to the story. After each person has shared and hands the ball to the next, they should make sure to hold on to one part of the string so that a circle is formed, connecting all in the group to each other. When the string makes it all the way around, close with a prayer of thanks for the connections shared and for the ties that bind the group as you go out into the world. (This is a good activity to use during the closing prayer of any session. Keep it in mind for future gatherings.)

Things to Ponder

This story is really about Simeon and Anna, as they represent the faithfulness and the expectation Israel has for the promised Messiah. There is great joy in them as they respond to the baby Jesus! Hopefully the youth can see the story through the eyes of Simeon and Anna. Yet the session may also trigger other issues in the youth and their connection to the story. Be aware of the possible family and parent issues that may come up from the experience of this story. Also look for signs of youth struggling with self-image issues or expectations in school or at home that they are struggling to meet.

Looking Ahead

Be sure to look through the session early enough in your preparation to allow you time to gather the resources you will need. You may want to check the classroom ahead of time to make sure the Bible study helps that you think will be useful are there.

~~~~~~

Birth Announcement

Name: _____

Birth Date: _____

Celebration of Life

Footprints

Encounter with the Baby Jesus

Reactions and Revelations

Simeon

What I said or heard . . .

What I thought or felt . . .

Mary

What I said or heard . . .

What I thought or felt . . .

Joseph

What I said or heard . . .

What I thought or felt . . .

Anna

What I said or heard . . .

What I thought or felt . . .

You

What I hear in the story . . .

What I think and feel about the story . . .

15. The Anointing at Bethany

Bible Story: Mark 14:3-9

Lauren Ng-Kushner

A Story behind the Story

The story of Jesus' anointing at Bethany is told in each of the three Synoptic Gospels: Matthew, Mark, and Luke. They are called "synoptic" (syn, "together"; optic, "see") because of their many similarities. It is currently believed that Mark was written before Matthew and Luke, perhaps explaining why it lacks the detail they include. This particular passage begins two days before Passover and the Festival of Unleavened Bread. A plot to kill Jesus is already in the works, and Jesus is visiting the home of Simon the leper in Bethany.

What happened in Simon's home is as challenging to explore now as it was then. An outpouring of devotion and selflessness, like none of those present had ever seen before, warmed Jesus' heart and granted him the occasion to teach yet another lesson. Without hesitation, a woman (who remains unnamed in Mark's account of this story) poured a jar of expensive ointment over Jesus' head, much to the dismay of her spectators (the "some who were there" in Mark's account). They were angry at her apparent wastefulness, claiming that the ointment should have been sold instead, its profits distributed to the poor. But Jesus' response to this seemingly noble claim suggests that he knew all too well with whom he was speaking. It is interesting to note that the Gospel of John replaces the "some who were there" with Judas Iscariot. In that account, Judas's motive of thievery is specifically named (John 12:6).

Jesus was pleased by the woman's actions not because of selfishness or negligence to the poor but because of how she carried them out. She offered them without deliberation, rationalization, or a weighing of options. Jesus' words to the spectators—and to us—speak beyond the results of buying power, which are often detached from the true vitality of human experience. Rather, they speak to the results of unquantifiable love, to what really prepares an individual for service to others.

It is also instructive to note those few verses that occur directly preceding this story. Verses 1 and 2 of this chapter tell us of the chief priests and scribes beginning to speak of Jesus' death. Then Jesus is anointed, much as a body would be when embalmed after death. This story thus both prefigures Jesus' death and brings that death into the realm of the greatest love of all.

Enter the Story

Find some time to consider this story carefully, taking notes as you read and react.

Imagine yourself as an active participant in this story. How would you react to the woman's actions as one of the spectators? How would you react to Jesus' response? Can you imagine yourself as the woman? Why or why not?

- How does God want me to serve others?
- How am I supposed to serve God?
- Is it wrong to keep some material possessions for myself? Does that make me selfish?
- How do I love unconditionally without getting hurt?

YOU MAY NEED

- props for a dining room setting
- small container(s) of olive or vegetable oil
- napkins
- "Picture This" handouts
- writing utensils
- markers or crayons
- photos or drawings of a bottle, a broken bottle, and an eyedropper
- "My Cover Story" handouts
- newsprint
- paper
- Bibles
- Bible study aids, such as Bible commentaries, dictionaries, encyclopedias, etc.

Think about how this story applies to your life and how it may apply to the lives of youth. Are there modern-day examples of this story that may help youth to understand its relevance?

As we grow as children of God, the idea of putting our faith into action becomes more and more important—and difficult. With so much logic to consider and so many consequences to weigh, hesitancy can sometimes muddle our good intentions. Consider what Jesus is asking us to do in this story. How do we love selflessly, put our faith into action, and throw hesitancy to the wind, given the world we live in? Is this what he's asking us to do?

Pray for the youth and for the Spirit of God to touch their hearts as they explore this story within the context of their unique faith journeys.

Setting the Stage (10 minutes)

OPTION A

Needed: props for a dining room setting

With what space and props you have, turn the room into a dining room setting. Have chairs around the table for the youth to occupy as they arrive. As they enter the room, greet them as extremely important guests (welcome them by name, pull their chairs out for them, have personalized place cards at their table setting, etc.).

When everyone is seated around the table, ask them to discuss what it felt like to be given such preferential treatment. Then ask them what kinds of things they do to prepare

themselves—or their home—for an important guest.

Share with them that today's Bible story tells about Jesus going to visit the home of a man with leprosy—a disease that would have made the man an outcast of society. Yet Jesus showed only love to this man. Explain that while a person may prepare to host a visitor, that visitor must also prepare to enter the person's home—with love, understanding, and acceptance. Such is the example Jesus has set, and such is the relationship between God and each of us. If we open our hearts to God, God will enter with unconditional love.

OPTION B

Needed: a small container of olive or vegetable oil, napkins

Once the youth have gathered, ask them to think of a time when either they or someone they know did something rash just to benefit another person. When they've all recalled an instance, divide them into pairs or groups of three to share their stories.

After they finish, gather the entire group together and pass around the container of oil. As a silent activity, have each youth come into contact with the oil (by dipping a finger into it, rubbing it between fingers, etc.). Encourage them to think carefully about the sensations they are having as they do this.

When everyone has done this, ask them to share their feelings about the activity.

- What did the oil feel like?
- Does anyone want a napkin?
- Was it a messy activity or not?

After they've shared their thoughts, ask them to think about how their interaction with the oil could be a metaphor for their relationship with God. Discuss their thoughts to this question as well. Explain that all of these questions and answers may be helpful in interpreting the biblical story they are about to hear.

Telling the Story
(10–15 minutes)
OPTION A
Needed: Bibles
Read the entire story of Mark 14:3-9 out loud to the group. Read slowly and deliberately, asking the youth to listen to the basics of the story. Read it again, but this time ask them to pay close attention to the words (the verbs, the adjectives, the emotions being displayed, etc.). Read it a third time, asking them to pick out the sentence or phrase or single word that stands out to them the most. Tell the group that you will read it a fourth time, and that you want them to stand when they hear the word(s) upon which they've chosen to focus.

After this last reading, invite class members to share with the group what word(s) they stood up for and why, allowing students the option to pass if they should so choose. If the group is large, you may want to divide them into smaller groups to discuss their choices. Consider beginning the sharing portion by saying a little about which part of the Scripture story stood out to you in your own study of it—or if something different stood out for you in this reading of it than had when you first studied it in preparation for the class. Your sharing may help make the youth more comfortable in their own sharing.

OPTION B
Needed: "Picture This" handouts, writing utensils, Bibles
Give the participants writing and coloring utensils and copies of the "Picture This" handout. Read Mark 14:3-9 at least twice as the youth fill in the cells of the cartoon strip. Have some Bibles available in case they want to refer to the passage as they draw.

When everyone has finished, have them form small groups to compare and discuss their drawings. If there's time, gather the whole group together again and open it up for discussion. You may want to offer the following questions to prompt conversation:
■ Which parts of the story did you choose to illustrate and why?
■ What was it like to create the visuals for this story?
■ Was it difficult?
■ What kinds of emotions did you try to capture in your drawings?

Reacting to the Story
(10–15 minutes)
OPTION A
Needed: Bibles, paper, writing utensils
Divide the group into two teams for a friendly debate. Assign one team the task of defending the "some who were there" at Simon's house (those who said that the oil should have been sold to benefit the poor). Assign the other team the task of

defending the woman who poured the oil over Jesus' head. Have each team prepare a presentation of their points for the other. Make sure they have Bibles available for reference to the Scripture during their preparations, as well as paper and writing utensils for any notes they may want to make.

Allow two or three minutes per team for their defense presentation. If you've got time and a large group, consider having a handful of class members act as "jury" for the trial, passing judgment at the end. Discuss the presentations as an entire group after both teams have presented.

OPTION B
Needed: Bibles, photos or drawings of a bottle, a broken bottle, and an eyedropper
One source suggests understanding the ointment as a metaphor for personality.[1] Within the framework of this metaphor, discuss with the group what it means for the woman to pour the ointment over Jesus' head without reservation.

Show the group the three pictures. (You could use the real thing for the bottles and eyedropper, but be cautious of the danger of having actual broken glass in the room.) Ask them to think about which picture best represents their own personality as they relate to others. Are they a closed bottle that has never been opened? Are they a broken bottle with the contents poured out and shared with others? Are they an eyedropper that lets only a bit out at a time, slowly and cautiously? If some youth would like to share

their reflections, have them do so, but be sensitive and respectful toward those who refrain.

Have the youth reread Mark 14:3-9 and try to think of a time when either they or someone they know exhibited the kind of servant attitude the woman did. Have those who would like to share do so.

Connecting to the Story (10–15 minutes)
OPTION A
Needed: "My Cover Story" handouts, writing utensils, including crayons or markers
Give everyone a copy of the "My Cover Story" handout and ask the group to take some time to complete it. Encourage them to use their imaginations! When everyone has finished, form pairs and have youth share their cover stories with one another. If there's time, gather the group back together again and have a discussion surrounding questions such as:
■ What, if anything, did you learn about yourself through this exercise?
■ What did you learn about your partner through his or her sharing with you?
■ What did Jesus mean when he said the woman's acts would be told in remembrance of her?
■ What acts of yours would you like to have told in remembrance of you? Are there any you would prefer not to be remembered by?

Explain that we don't have to accomplish newsworthy feats in order to be remembered by our families, communities, and God. We are each a unique creation, newsworthy in our own right because of the loving God who made us in the divine image.

OPTION B
Needed: newsprint, marker
Explain to the group that based on the current U.S. minimum wage of $5.15 per hour, three hundred denarii would have an equivalent buying power of $12,360.00 today. Write the following questions on newsprint and have the group form pairs to discuss them, taking turns as questioner and answerer:
■ If you had $12,360.00 to spend on yourself, how would you spend it?
■ If you had $12,360.00 to spend on a person or persons other than yourself, how would you spend it?
■ What is the most memorable gift you ever received? Why is it so memorable?
■ What is the most memorable gift you've given to someone else? Why is it so memorable?
■ Why do you think the woman spent so much money on ointment?
■ Do you think you would have agreed with the people who complained about it if you were there? Why or why not?
■ Why do you think Jesus approved of her spending it this way?

**Exploring the Story
(10–15 minutes)**
OPTION A
Needed: writing utensils, Bibles, Bible study aids
Form pairs and instruct the youth to write a question they have about the story at the top of a piece of

paper. Then have each person trade his or her piece of paper with the partner. After explaining what Bible study resources you've gathered and how they can be used, have each person research his or her partner's question. You may want to wander around the room, lending assistance to anyone who wants it. Be aware that some youth may have never used Bible study resources before, and so you may be able to help them by suggesting some creative approaches to using these resources.

When everyone has had significant time to research, have partners report their findings to each other. If there's time, allow volunteers to share their findings with the entire group.

OPTION B
Needed: writing utensils, paper, Bibles, Bible study aids (optional)
Form teams of three or four and have each team study the following stories in relationship to one another: Matthew 26:1-13, Mark 14:1-9, Luke 7:36-50, and John 12:1-8. Instruct them to look for such things as particular words that are different from one to the other, names of characters that might be different, any changes in context (looking at verses preceding and following the story to see the "where" and "when" and "what happened after" of the story), etc. Have each team determine one new insight as well as one new question they have about the story as a result of reading these other accounts.

After they've recorded their findings, each team will present to the entire group. Once every team has presented, open the floor for group discussion. If you have time, it would enhance the study if you made Bible study resources (such as those mentioned in Option A) available to the youth for them to look into the questions they have raised. A particularly helpful avenue of exploration might be to look into the historical audiences (time frame, location, and community of the Gospel writer) of each of the Gospels, and whether the differences in audience might account for the differences in the Gospel accounts of this story. In either case, it's a fruitful discussion for youth to have about the nature of the Bible itself, in terms of differences in the same story recorded in different places. Why might that be? What does it mean in terms of our belief in the Bible stories themselves?

Living the Story (5–10 minutes)

OPTION A

Form a circle and thank the youth for their openness and enthusiasm during the session. Invite each person to share with the group something they've learned about themselves or their relationship with Christ as a result of today's activities. Do they have any better understanding of servanthood? Do they have any better understanding of discipleship? Did today's Scripture story give them any new insights into the nature of our relationship with Jesus?

You may want to begin this time of sharing with a thought of your own. This will communicate to the youth your willingness and desire to be open with them and will enable them to share more comfortably with the entire group.

When everyone who wants to share has done so, close the session with a prayer or a song that expresses thanks to God for bringing your group together in relationship with one another and with God.

OPTION B

Needed: cruet or jar of vegetable oil, one small container of oil for each youth (optional)

If you happen to be doing this session during Lent, you may want to state the significance of this Bible story within the larger context of Mark's Passion narrative (Jesus' last days before his crucifixion and resurrection). Whether or not you are in Lent, explain to the group that in the Bible, an anointing of oil is a symbol of a covenant between God and God's people. In today's Bible story, the woman anoints Jesus as a fulfillment of God's covenant with us that Jesus would be crucified so that we would have everlasting life.

Form a circle and explain that we can express our Christian covenant (or promise) to one another and God by anointing each other with oil. Dip your finger in the container of oil and anoint the person to your right by painting a cross on her or his hand. Pass the oil around the circle until the last youth has anointed you. If you have the resource to purchase small bottles of oil for each youth (available at many Christian bookstores), then distribute those now to each participant, asking them to keep their container somewhere prominent in their homes (on the dresser, near their toothbrushes, near their place at the kitchen table) to remind them of Christ's presence in their lives each time they see the container.

Close with prayer, thanking God for bringing your group together in a covenantal relationship with one another and with God.

Things to Ponder

This Bible story is likely to confront youth with the realities surrounding their relationships with others and with God. It is also a story that alludes to the death of Jesus on the cross. Be prepared for all types of responses during the session, keeping in mind that the seeming lack of response is still a valid and noteworthy reaction. Consider which youth were hesitant to participate during certain activities. Is there a way that you can engage those youth—or better understand them—during the next session? How about outside of the larger group? Or in a one-on-one conversation?

Looking Ahead

Depending on which option you choose, you may need to find large sheeting or banner felt for creating a banner. Using an old sheet would be sufficient, but you may also want to check fabric stores, craft stores, or art supply stores for large pieces of felt.

Note

1. *The Interpreter's Bible*, vol. VII. Leander E. Keck, ed. (Nashville: Abingdon-Cokesbury, 1951), p. 868.

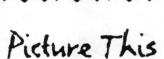

Picture This

As you listen to this Bible story, fill in the cells of this cartoon strip with illustrations that tell the story. It's not necessary to illustrate the entire passage or fill in each cell. As you draw, pay close attention to the emotions, sensory experiences, and powerful language used in the story.

My Cover Story

You've just won Millennium *magazine's Person of the Century Award for your amazing accomplishment of peace, love, and compassion. Congratulations! You will always be remembered for what you've done for the sake of God's world! Illustrate your cover below.*

Millennium

Congratulations to _____,

Millennium **magazine's Person of the Century for**

_____.

16. Thomas

Bible Story: John 20:19-29

Sandra DeMott Hasenauer

A Story behind the Story

Thomas has gotten a bad rap. You see, all these years he's gone by the epithet "doubting Thomas," as if no one else had any misgivings about Jesus' resurrection. The implication is that everyone else must have immediately said, "Well, of course!" when presented with the message that the crucified Jesus lived. Thomas, however, had to take a few days to think about it.

Well, I think it's time that Thomas was allowed some leeway. When we look at the verses immediately preceding our Scripture story, Mary wasn't too sure what was going on (John 20:13-16) until Jesus made it crystal clear to her. Even after Peter and the nameless "other disciple" had visited the empty tomb, Jesus still showed them his hands and his side when he appeared to them the next day (John 20:20). In fact, we are told directly that Thomas wasn't with them when this happened. Why should we assume that Thomas should automatically believe just based on the other disciples' word for it? They didn't have to only rely on word of mouth—Jesus had already supplied them with the same evidence.

Thomas has stood an awful lot of bashing over the years: "Don't be like Thomas! He doubted!" In point of fact, upon closer reading, it would seem that the story is less about doubt versus unquestioning belief as it is about Jesus' role in our belief. Jesus worked with first Mary, then the disciples, and then Thomas to move them from unbelief to belief. Isn't that the same task set before Jesus with each of us? Our journey as Christians is a constant move from unbelief to belief. Jesus' tremendous love for us, his disciples, is to offer us himself as living proof of God's loving kindness for the world. Jesus offered each of the faithful in these three stories what they needed to believe. And then he went on to suggest that those who do not see and yet believe are blessed. This is not a castigation of those who need to see but rather is a blessing offered to those of us, generations later, who are in the position of having to believe without seeing.

Perhaps, when our eyes are opened as Thomas's were, we will have the courage, the strength, and the unbridled joy to cause us to shout, "My Lord and my God!"

Enter the Story

This is the type of story best read with some quiet, meditative music playing in the background and a candle lit. Allow yourself some time to bask in God's presence as you enter into the experience of the story. Pray for your faith to be strengthened through these words, and offer up your own areas of unbelief as you focus your attention on God's message through Scripture.

Setting the Stage (5–10 minutes)

OPTION A

As the youth start entering the room, stand at the door and rush them in their entering. Pull them gently, glancing into the hallway or space outside your meeting area nervously. Encourage them to whisper, not talk out loud, and do your best to get them nervous without knowing why they're feeling nervous. Once everyone is in, quickly close the door, pretending to lock it. (For safety reasons, however, do not actually lock the door.) If you have windows in your meeting space, rush over to the windows and close the blinds.

Once you have set the scene, be quick to reassure the youth that nothing is wrong in the church. However, explain that the disciples must have had to behave like this as they gathered together in the days following Jesus' crucifixion. Suspicion of Jesus' followers was running high—they were quickly becoming considered enemies of the state. Explain that today's Scripture story took place in a locked room, with disciples hidden away for fear of their lives.

Note: Recent historical events may make this type of activity a little too real for youth, so be aware of particular sensitivities to issues of fear and safety and adapt the activity as may be necessary.

OPTION B
Once the youth have arrived and you've spent a few moments greeting each other, inform the youth that you will now offer them a series of statements about beliefs. They are to move toward one end of the room or the other based on whether or not they believe the statement. They may also choose to stand anywhere in the middle of the two ends, based on where on the

spectrum of belief they may fall. Once they are there, after each statement, ask the youth to say briefly why they responded the way they did—in other words, what does it take to make them believe?

Use the following choices, but feel free to add some of your own.
■ Santa Claus comes on Christmas Eve.
■ The world is round.
■ I can chew gum and walk at the same time.
■ There is no such thing as a free lunch.
■ Noah built an ark.
■ God exists.

After you've had some time for the youth to consider what it takes for them to believe something, explain that today's story is about some disciples' struggles to believe and what sort of evidence they're offered.

Telling the Story (5–10 minutes)
OPTION A
Needed: Bibles
Break the class into three groups, or if you have a smaller class, have the whole class do all three parts of the following activity. Explain to the class that each time they hear the name Jesus in the reading, they are to cheer wildly. Each time they hear the name Thomas, they are to shout, "I'll believe it when I see it!" Finally, each time they hear the word "disciples," they should stand up and make a cross with their forearms in front of their chests. (If you've divided into three groups, assign each group one of these, and have the groups stand whenever they do their assigned part and then immediately sit again.)

■ Why can't I have visible proof that God exists?
■ How am I supposed to believe in something that makes no sense?
■ Am I wrong to doubt?
■ Can I truly call Jesus "my Lord and my God"?

YOU MAY NEED
■ Bibles
■ drawing paper
■ colored pencils, crayons, markers, or other drawing implements
■ Play-Doh or other modeling clay
■ "I Believe . . ." handouts
■ writing utensils
■ "History Repeats Itself" handouts
■ newsprint or chalkboard
■ markers or chalk
■ worship planning resources, such as Bibles, hymnals or songbooks, prayer books, and liturgy books
■ CD player and Christian music CDs (optional)
■ blank or scrap paper
■ large fabric for banner, such as sheeting or banner felt
■ scissors (multiple sharp pairs, if possible, for cutting fabric)
■ glue
■ markers
■ assorted decorative supplies such as glitter, feathers, puff balls, etc.

Read through the Scripture, and encourage the youth to be as loud and raucous as you can get away with being in your classroom without disturbing anyone else. In fact, if you have a few extra minutes and really want to get the class going, emphasize the different names or say them two or three times in a row, to get the class cheering, shouting, or standing and forming the cross, quickly and more loudly. For example, verse 24 might be read as "But Thomas . . . Thomas . . . THOMAS! (who was called the Twin). . . . " And then later: "when Jesus . . . I said, Jesus! . . . I say it again, JESUS! . . . came. So the other disciples—wait, did I say disciples? I mean . . . DISCIPLES! . . . told him. . . . "

OPTION B
Needed: Bibles
Find two volunteers—one who will read the words of Jesus and a second who will read the words of Thomas. The rest of the class will read, in unison, the words of the disciples. Give everyone a chance to skim the Scripture silently first, and especially encourage the "Jesus" and "Thomas" readers to consider appropriate tones of voice for their parts.

Read the Scripture together, with you serving as narrator. Make sure the readers all do their parts loudly enough for everyone to hear.

After the reading is done, and if you have a few extra minutes, feel free to ask the class to consider if any of the people speaking could have used a different tone of voice for any of their persons' statements. How much meaning is conveyed in tone of voice? If you're able to have

this discussion, consider reading the Scripture story again, using some of these other inflections in some of the statements.

Reacting to the Story (10–15 minutes)
OPTION A
Needed: Bibles, drawing paper, colored pencils, crayons, markers, and other drawing implements
Make the drawing supplies available to the youth, and invite them each to choose a scene in the story that they would like to depict in a drawing or cartoon. Encourage those youth who despair of their artistic talent that stick figures can often be just as expressive as complicated artistic renderings. Suggest that they refer to the story in their Bibles as they choose their scene, looking at the Scripture to see as many details about their chosen scene as they can find. What characters are present? What might be the expressions on their faces? What are their surroundings?

They may not choose to focus their drawing on every aspect of the scene, of course. One youth may want to draw only the expression on Thomas's face when the disciples first tell him of Jesus' resurrection. Another might draw Jesus' hand with its wound. They may choose whatever aspect of the story they'd like to draw.

After giving them several minutes to finish their work, instruct the youth to get in line (holding their drawings) in consecutive order of the story. The youth who chose to draw the disciples locked in their house in verse 19 would stand at one side of the room, and the student who drew Jesus saying, "Blessed are those who have not seen," would be standing at the other end of the room, with the other youth stretched out between them in order. If more than one youth drew a scene, have them stand together. Go through the drawings in consecutive order, being sure to compliment everyone's drawings.

OPTION B
Needed: Play-Doh or other modeling clay, Bibles
Give each youth a golf-ball-sized mound of Play-Doh or modeling clay. Ask them to review the story silently to themselves, paying particular attention to how they imagine Thomas's face to appear at various points of the story. Invite them each to use the clay to sculpt Thomas's face and his expression in verses 24-25 as they imagine it, and share it with each other. (Do this in pairs or triads if you have a larger class.) After they've shared, have them move on in the story and change their sculptured face to show Thomas's expression in verses 28-29, then share it with each other again.

Connecting to the Story
(10–15 minutes)
OPTION A
Needed: "I Believe . . ." handouts, writing utensils, Bibles
Give a copy of the "I Believe . . ." handout and a writing utensil to each person. Make sure they have access to a Bible. Give them several minutes to fill out the handout, then invite them to get into pairs or triads to share as much of their response as they feel comfortable.

OPTION B
Have the youth get comfortable. Make sure they are far enough away from other students to cut down on distractions. Invite them to close their eyes and breathe slowly, consciously relaxing themselves and focusing on your voice. Lead them in a guided reflection on the Scripture, making sure your voice is slow and easy to listen to.

If you enjoy creating guided reflections on your own, feel free to do so—the idea is to have the youth put themselves into the room where Thomas and the disciples are and to experience the story more fully that way. You may use the following reflection as a guide, with the bracketed statements serving as clues for ways to flesh out the reflection yourself: *Imagine the room in which the disciples sit. They have gathered for a meal together.* [Fill in details, such as the table and food laid upon it.] *Look around the table—there are Peter and James and John and Philip . . .* [Fill in the names of the other disciples, leaving out the Judas who betrayed, of course.] *Put yourself there. Imagine yourself sitting among them, listening in to their conversation. The disciples are afraid—they've got the door locked because someone might come after one of them next. But they're not quite as afraid as before—they've seen Jesus! You can hear the buzz of excited comments and whispers. There's a soft knock on the door, and Andrew jumps up to carefully open it. Thomas slips in and takes a seat across the table from you. "We've seen the Lord!" exclaims Bartholomew, unable to contain his excitement. You see Thomas's face. . . .* Continue to make the story come alive for the youth, right through Jesus' statement in verse 29.

When you've finished the reflection, invite the youth to share their experiences. Did something strike them in the scene differently from when they first read it? What did they imagine the disciples doing? Thomas? Would they have had the same reaction?

Exploring the Story
(10–15 minutes)
OPTION A
Needed: "History Repeats Itself" handouts, writing utensils, Bibles
Give each youth a copy of the "History Repeats Itself" handout and a writing utensil. Make sure they have access to the Bible. Invite them to take a few moments to read through the information on the handout, look up the Scriptures mentioned, and respond to the questions at the end. After they've done so, invite them to share their responses in pairs or triads as they feel comfortable.

If you have a few extra minutes, bring the group back together and ask if knowing some of that historical information puts a different light on the Scripture story for them. Say something like, *Imagine what it would be like to read this passage if you were a person undergoing persecution for your faith somewhere in the world today. Would it make it feel any different? Would you interpret it differently?*

OPTION B
Needed: Bibles, newsprint and markers or chalkboard and chalk
Have one youth read again John 20:22, and invite a second youth to read Matthew 28:19-20 (often referred to as the Great Commission). On a newsprint or chalk-board, put the two Scriptures at the top of side-by-side columns and compare them. What are the similarities between the two? The differences? Could they both be considered commissions? (You may need to invite youth to look the word up in a dictionary.)

Does the John 20 passage mean that we should judge people's sins and decide who's right or wrong? If so, how do we do that? If not, what does it mean?

Compare these passages with your church. How is your congregation carrying out Jesus' commission? Where might it need to do more? Consider using a second piece of newsprint or a clean section of chalkboard to list activities of your church under categories that would fit your comparison of the Scriptures—a category that would reflect your discussion about the remission of sins, one about making disciples, one about teaching, etc. If you've got time, have the youth brainstorm an activity they could plan to carry out that would fulfill part of the commission.

Living the Story
(5–10 minutes)
OPTION A
Needed: worship planning resources, paper, writing utensils, CD player and Christian music CDs (optional)
Invite the youth to create a brief worship service that would reflect their study and conversation today. What might be the theme of the service? Remind them of the different topics they have discussed during the session, and help them to decide which theme they feel is most appropriate for a closing

worship service. Invite them to choose or write prayers that might be used and find songs they'd like to sing together. If you have access to a CD player and some Christian CDs, invite them to choose music for prelude or postlude music.

You may want to divide your class into smaller groups if it feels appropriate. Each group could be assigned one portion of the service to plan (one group to find music, one to write prayers, etc.).

Consider whether you would like to include such things as Communion, a foot washing, or some other ritual of faith that would be significant to the youth. Be sure to leave enough time to actually share in your planned worship together.

OPTION B
Needed: banner-making supplies (e.g., sheeting or banner felt), fabric scissors, glue, markers, assorted decorative supplies, including glitter, feathers, puff balls, etc.
Invite the group to work together to create a banner that depicts Jesus' statement "Blessed are those who have not seen and yet have come to believe" (John 20:29). The youth should first sketch out their idea on scrap paper or a chalkboard, then work together to bring their banner into reality. Make sure everyone has a role—for example, even if they're not artistic, they can cut out pieces of felt that someone else has outlined for them. However, encourage everyone to have input into the plan of the design rather than leaving it up to the recognized "artist" of the group. Make sure they read through the Scripture story one more time as they are creating their design—they might

choose to use an image from the story itself within their plan.

Once the banner is done, be sure to find a prominent place in the church to display it so that the entire congregation can admire it and be blessed by its message.

Things to Ponder
Teenagers, like all of us, struggle with issues of doubt and faith. It is a necessary part of our faith journey and one that will recur continuously throughout our lives. However, youth often feel "wrong" for doubting, or they will try to make others feel so. On the flip side are those youth who choose to express strong disbelief as part of their own rebellion against parents or a need to be different. Be sure to reassure all your youth that doubt is a natural part of faith, and don't let the rebellious ones put you off. Don't belittle their comments—they may truly be having their own faith struggles. But a lack of shocked dismay on your part will tend to quiet those who are simply spouting off for the sake of trying to rile people. Instead, try to turn it into a good conversation starter!

Looking Ahead
Depending on which options you choose, you may need to locate a copy of the movie *The Shawshank Redemption* and have it cued to the appropriate place. You may need to do some research on the global persecution of Christians and imprisonment of prisoners of conscience and be prepared to present that information to the class. You might also need to invite youth to bring in a music CD, as described in the next session's "Setting the Stage."

I Believe . . .

Lots of people express different types of belief in Scripture. Read the passages below and respond to the questions that follow.

Mark 9:14-28

What does verse 24 say, specifically? Write it here:

What do you think the father meant by this?

Have you ever had times when you felt like you had belief and unbelief at the same time?

Can what the father says be considered a prayer? Why or why not? If so, is this a good prayer? Is it one you might pray?

John 2:23, 4:39,42

Why do the people in John 2:23 believe in Jesus?

Why do the people in John 4:39 believe in Jesus?

Why do these same people in John 4:42 now believe in Jesus?

What did Thomas need in order to believe that Jesus had been resurrected (John 20:25)?

Into which of these categories would you place yourself? In other words, what would you need in order to believe in Jesus?

History Repeats Itself

The Disciples

John 20:19 mentions that the disciples had the doors of the house where they met "locked for fear of the Jews." After all, Jesus had just been crucified in the manner the Roman government used to execute its political prisoners. In Roman eyes, Jesus and his followers were part of an anti-Roman political movement—talk of "kings" and "kingdoms" threatened them, regardless of whether those kingdoms were heavenly or otherwise. The Jewish leaders had worked out a relatively peaceful coexistence with the Romans. Yes, the Romans had conquered their land and were an occupying force, but the Jews had managed to be left alone for the most part. They had received some leniency for their people by cooperating with the Romans where necessary. Jesus and his followers threatened that uneasy balance. So the Jewish leaders were instrumental in turning Jesus in, believing they were doing the best for the safety of the people in their care. The disciples, having witnessed Jesus' death, were positive they'd be next.

The Audience of the Gospel of John

No one knows for sure, of course, but there's plenty of evidence to indicate that the Gospel of John was put into writing sometime around A.D. 90. By that time, the Jesus movement was becoming more crystallized as something significantly different from Judaism. When Jesus' initial disciples first began preaching and making converts (as we see in the Book of Acts), they believed they were still Jews. In fact, there are several stories of their slow and sometimes reluctant realization that God intended them to preach to the Gentiles *as well as* to the Jews. At first, they truly thought they were a movement within the Jewish faith. The Jewish leaders recognized otherwise—this was something different. Acts and John both reflect the growing division between Judaism and the infant movement of Christianity (read Acts 6:9-14 for an example), culminating in Jesus followers being expelled from the synagogue. It was a painful time for everyone, and the writer of the Gospel of John expressed some of this pain and anger through his comments on "the Jews." At the same time, Christians were being persecuted sporadically by the Roman government. Again, the Book of Acts describes some martyrdoms (read Acts 7:54-60 for an example) and several arrests. John's audience may have felt a similar fear to that of the disciples. The writer of John would have wanted to strengthen their faith by reminding them of Jesus' peace and love, offered to the disciples in that room in John 20.

Do you need to be reassured of Jesus' presence? Why? Do you feel that reassurance? How?

17. Lydia's Conversion

Bible Story: Acts 16:11-40

Rene Rodgers Jensen

A Story behind the Story

The story in Acts 16 illustrates how Paul typically began a church in a new community. In most parts of the Roman Empire there lived Gentiles who were familiar with Judaism and attracted to many of its tenets, such as the belief in one God, and its ethical teachings. These Gentiles were called God-fearers or God-worshipers. Even though they were attracted to Judaism, these God-worshipers were reluctant to become actual converts because of the strictures of being obedient to all the demands of Jewish laws. The God-worshipers were among the earliest converts to Christianity because Christianity offered all that they found attractive in Judaism without the additional burden of Jewish law.

In Philippi, Paul encountered one of these God-worshipers, a wealthy businesswoman named Lydia. She and her household were baptized, and Paul and his companions were invited to stay in her home. All the earliest churches were in the homes of well-to-do converts like Lydia.

From there the story takes a dramatic turn. A young slave girl who was possessed by a spirit that gave her the power to divine the future began to follow Paul and the others around, shouting that they were servants of the Most High. Paul eventually became so angry that he cast out the spirit. This is a puzzling part of the story. Was Paul angry at the ruckus the girl was creating? Or was he angry over her economic exploitation? The Scripture is unclear. At any rate, the slave girl's owners were enraged because she could no longer make them money. They caused Paul and Silas to be thrown into prison, accusing them of causing an uproar in the city.

But Paul and Silas used their imprisonment as an opportunity for witness that led to the conversion of their jailer and his family. Meanwhile, because Paul's Roman citizenship (which afforded him some legal protection not given to noncitizens) had come to light, the men were released.

There is a lot going on in this story. There is Lydia, who is the founder of the church in Philippi. (Indeed, throughout Paul's letters and in the Book of Acts, it is clear that women played a prominent role in the early church.) There is the dramatic story of the slave girl and her greedy owners. Then there is the exciting story of Paul and Silas's imprisonment and the conversion of their jailer. Salvation flows throughout this story—God's will at work in the most surprising of places!

Enter the Story

Read the Scripture passage through. Note that when Paul cured the slave girl of the spirit who possessed her, the slave own- ers became very angry. Instead of rejoicing that this young girl, who had been tormented her whole life by demon possession, had at last been cured, they became angry because they had lost a source of steady income. Religion had gotten in the way of their making a living.

Of course, none of us are slave owners, but how often do we think of our faith in relation to how we earn our living? Do we keep our faith separate from our values about money, or do we let our faith shape how we make a living and how we use our financial resources? Reflect on these questions for yourself as you prepare the lesson.

Think about your students. Some of them are beginning to think about choosing a career. Some of them have jobs that give them some financial resources. How can you help them see that their faith is not just a matter of Sunday mornings but a total life choice?

Setting the Stage (5–10 minutes)

OPTION A
Needed: CD player, CDs of various music styles
If you planned on using this option, you have asked youth to bring in a CD that they like to listen to when they are feeling down. In case no one remembers to bring a CD, have on hand some CDs or tapes of your own. Choose a variety of music that people might conceivably listen to when they are depressed or sad— upbeat and celebrative, contemplative, mournful. A mix of sacred and secular music would work well.

Ask youth who brought CDs to play them. Ask them to explain why they listen to this music when they are down.

Invite others in the group to respond. Is this the kind of music they would like to listen to? Why or why not?

Alternatively, or to supplement the music that the kids bring in, play some of the music you have brought. Ask the youth to respond to the music. Ask questions such as:
- Which kind of music would cheer you up?
- Would any of the music make you feel more depressed? If so, why?
- Why do people so often find comfort and inspiration in music?

OPTION B
Needed: Video of The Shawshank Redemption, *TV and VCR*
Give a brief background of the story of the movie. Andy Dufresne is a man unjustly convicted of murdering his wife. He has been imprisoned in Shawshank Prison, where he is surrounded by violent men. Among the most violent are those who run the prison. Nevertheless, Andy makes a few friends, including Red, who is the narrator. Andy also strives to make the prison a slightly more humane place by working to get a better prison library.

Cue the video up to the point where Andy locks himself in the warden's office and plays Mozart over the loudspeakers to the prison (this is roughly 1:06 into the video). Play through the scene in the cafeteria in which Andy says that they can't take Mozart away from him because he still has Mozart in his head and in his heart.

Ask the youth to tell why they thought it was so important for Andy to play Mozart, despite the severe punishment he knew he would receive.

POSSIBLE YOUTH CONTACT POINTS
- What is imprisoning me?
- How does Christ set me free?
- How much am I willing to risk for my faith?

YOU MAY NEED
- CD player
- Favorite CDs, including a variety of music styles
- *The Shawshank Redemption* video
- TV and VCR
- Bibles
- chalkboard or newsprint
- chalk or markers
- writing utensils
- paper
- construction paper
- scissors
- Scotch tape
- information from the Internet on persecution
- computer with Internet connection (optional)
- "Paul's Missionary Journeys" handouts
- Bible atlas (optional)
- biblical land wall maps (optional)
- "Snapshots of Women in the Young Church" handouts
- candle
- matches or lighter
- basket or offering tray

- What was the effect of that music on the other prisoners? Why?
- Why does Andy think music is especially important in a place like prison?

Telling the Story
(5–10 minutes)
OPTION A

Needed: Bibles

Hand out the Bibles. Before reading the passage, ask individuals or pairs to pay particular attention to the following characters and be prepared to explain their behavior.

Have a volunteer or volunteers read Acts 16:11-40. Ask the following questions of those who were assigned the character:

- Lydia—Why do you become a Christian? What attracts you to this religion?
- Slave girl—Why did you follow Paul and the others around? How did you feel when they cast out the spirit that gave you the ability to tell the future?
- Slave owners—Why did you get so angry with Paul and Silas? Why did you want them thrown into jail?
- Jailer—What did you think when you heard Paul and Silas singing hymns in prison? Why did you try to kill yourself when you thought the prisoners had escaped? Why did you become a Christian? Would you have responded any differently if Paul and Silas had escaped when the earthquake came?

Ask the entire group to respond to the following questions about Paul and Silas:

- Why did you make the spirit come out of the slave girl?

- Why were you singing hymns while you were in prison?
- Why didn't you try to get away when the earthquake opened all the doors?
- Why did you save the jailer's life when he was working for the people who threw you into prison?

OPTION B

Needed: Bibles, chalkboard and chalk or newsprint and markers

Divide the class into two groups. Assign one group the job of telling the story from the perspective of the slave owners. Ask the second group to tell the story from the perspective of the jailer.

Read Acts 16:11-40. On a chalkboard or sheet of newsprint, write the following questions:

- What happened?
- Who was involved?
- Why did you react the way you did?
- How did you feel?

Give each of the two groups a few minutes to tell the story from the perspective assigned to them. Have them use the questions as a guide for telling their story. The group assigned the perspective of the slave owners should tell what happened from 16:16-22. Those telling the story from the viewpoint of the jailer should recount what happened in 16:23-34.

Reacting to the Story
(15–20 minutes)
OPTION A

Explain to the group that we see various kinds of salvation in this story. Have the group discuss the following questions:

- What does salvation mean in relationship to Lydia? What, if anything, did she risk by becoming a Christian?
- From what was the slave girl saved? How was her life changed by her encounter with Paul?
- From what did the slave owners need to be saved? What was the most important thing in their lives?
- From what were Paul and Silas saved?
- How was the jailer saved? How do you think his life was different from that time forward?

Ask the group to discuss the different kinds of salvation. Then discuss these questions:
- What comes to mind when you hear the words "salvation" or "saved"?
- When have you experienced a sense of being saved from a difficult circumstance or frightening situation?
- With whom do you most identify in the story?
- In verse 30 the jailer asks, "What must I do to be saved?" How would you answer that question if someone asked it of you today?

OPTION B
Needed: writing utensils and paper or newsprint and markers
This passage from Acts has an over-the-top quality. The encounters with the slave girl and her owners, the jailer, and the magistrates all make for dramatic stories.

The Tabloid Bible by Nick Page recounts biblical stories as if they were appearing in a tabloid newspaper. For instance, the story of Pentecost is headlined,

Followers of Jesus Filled with Wind
Disciples Speak Different Languages

Paul's conversion is headlined,

Chaos on Damascus Road
Did Aliens Cause Multi-chariot
 Pileup?

The story of Jesus feeding the five thousand has this headline:

Jesus Feeds Five Thousand
"He Cut the Bread Very Thin,"
 Claim Skeptics[1]

Invite the class to come up with tabloid headlines for the different amazing events in Acts 16. If you have a large group, divide into two or three small groups, give them writing utensils and paper, and have them come up with their own headlines. Have them share the headlines with the whole group. If yours is a small group, work together and write the tabloid headlines on newsprint.

Connecting to the Story (10–15 minutes)
OPTION A
Needed: construction paper, scissors, writing utensils, Scotch tape
Explain to the youth that in this story from Acts, Paul and Silas were thrown in jail. That is one kind of prison. But other people were also imprisoned. What was imprisoning the slave girl? What was imprisoning the slave owners? The magistrates? The jailer?

Give every participant a piece of paper and a pen or pencil. Ask them to cut the paper in strips to make a paper chain. Then divide the class into pairs and have each pair write what might imprison someone on the slips of paper—one word per slip. Tape the slips of paper into a link to form a paper chain.

Ask the youth to tell what they wrote on their chains. Then tape all the chains together and wrap them around the whole group. Ask them to name what can set people free from these chains. Then have a mass breakout! Celebrate the breakout by high-fiving and cheering one another.

OPTION B
Needed: current Internet information on persecution, computer with Internet connection (optional)
In the United States and Canada, we have a tendency to take our freedom of religion and freedom of speech for granted. It is easy to forget that Christians are still being persecuted and imprisoned for their faith in many countries around the world. Persons who speak out against oppressive governments are often jailed.

Either ahead of time on your own or during class with the youth, if you have access to an Internet connection in your church, look on the Internet for information about countries where persons are being persecuted for their beliefs. A search with key words "Christians imprisoned" or "Christians persecuted" should reveal some current information. Amnesty International usually has good information about prisoners of conscience. Share these stories with the youth if you've gotten them ahead of time, or have the youth note the headlines and brief synopses of the stories if they're finding them during class.

Christians do not face overt persecution or imprisonment in our country, but that does not mean that our culture always values the Christian faith. Have the group list ways in which following Christ can mean making a choice that is contrary to the values of the culture. How can making those choices lead to a kind of persecution?

Note: If you have time, you may want to include a conversation about Christians' persecution of other faiths historically and what like that might be still happening in the world today.

Exploring the Story (10–15 minutes)
OPTION A
Needed: " Paul's Missionary Journeys" handouts, Bibles, Bible maps or atlas (optional)
Explain that the Book of Acts tells the story of the expansion of the church. Christianity began in the land of Israel, a rather obscure country under the governance of Rome. By the end of the first century, Christianity had spread to almost every corner of the Roman Empire, which was most of the known world of that time.

That spread was due primarily to the missionary work of the apostle Paul. Paul began as Saul, a persecutor of Christians. He even participated in the death of Stephen, the first Christian martyr. But while he was on his way to Damascus, intent on arresting the Christians there, he had a vision of the risen Christ that caused him to become as zealous in preaching the gospel as he had previously been in persecuting the followers of Christ.

Paul's passion for preaching the good news of Jesus Christ resulted in the rapid spread of Christianity throughout the Roman Empire. Paul saw himself as the apostle to the Gentiles. By the end of his ministry, Gentile Christianity was well on its way to becoming the dominant force in the young church.

Distribute copies of the handout "Paul's Missionary Journeys." You may also want to look at a Bible atlas as an additional resource. If your church has a good set of wall maps, you may want to use those maps to supplement the smaller maps. Many biblical map sets have a map devoted to Paul's missionary journeys.

Have the youth note the extent of the Roman Empire, then find Jerusalem on the map. Look for other familiar towns from the Scriptures, such as Bethlehem and Nazareth. Trace Paul's missionary journeys. Find Philippi. Look in the New Testament for the letters of Paul. Find other cities where he founded churches or to whom he wrote letters (Corinth, Thessalonica, Ephesus, Rome).

OPTION B
Needed: "Snapshots of Women in the Young Church" handouts, Bibles, writing utensils
In Acts 16:11-15 we read of the conversion of Lydia and the start of the Philippian church in her home. Many of the prominent persons in the early church were women. Have the youth look up the Scripture passages listed on the handout "Snapshots of Women in the Young Church" to find out more about the women in the first century

church. Ask the youth if they were aware that so many of the leaders of the early church were women. What is the role of women in your congregation?

Living the Story (10–15 minutes)
OPTION A
Needed: chalkboard and chalk or newsprint and marker, candle, matches or lighter, basket, slips of paper, writing utensils
To get started, ask questions such as these:
■ What happens if you say you are a Christian but act in an unchristian manner? What does that say to others?
■ What happens if you lead a good life and help others but never say you are a Christian? How will anyone know you are a follower of Jesus?

Next, ask the group:
■ Which is more important—what we say or what we do? Or, are they equally important in witnessing to someone else about our faith?

Paul and Silas witnessed to the jailer both by their actions and by their words. Have the group make a list of ways to witness to others about their faith. Some witnessing may be by words, some by actions.

Light the candle and place it on a table. Place the basket or tray beside it. Gather the group around the candle and ask them to think about the ways to share your faith that you have been discussing. Remind the youth that we are all Christians because someone told us about Jesus. If we stopped telling others about Jesus, in just a generation there would be no more

Christians. We have an obligation to pass the faith on to others.

Give each person a piece of paper and a pencil. Ask them to write on the paper one way they can witness their faith in the coming week. Have them place the paper in the basket as a way of making an offering to God. Offer a prayer of blessing and thanksgiving.

OPTION B
Needed: CD player, music CD
If you chose Option A under "Setting the Stage," close the session by returning to one of the pieces of music that you played at the beginning. Remind the group of how they identified this song as a source of comfort and strength when they are down. Ask them to name some of the challenges they will be facing in the coming week. Ask the group to name other ways they can find strength to face those challenges.

Close with prayer that names the challenges facing the members of the group and asking for God's strength and guidance in whatever may lie ahead in the coming days.

Things to Ponder
Soon after the session, reflect on what happened. Where did the youth seem to respond particularly well? What produced positive energy in the room? What didn't seem to work at all? Did any personal concerns or issues arise that need follow-up? If so, make a note to call or email in the coming week to check in on the youth. Reflect on your own leadership. Your own willingness to be open and vulnerable will help the youth be honest about their own feelings.

Looking Ahead
You may need to find a copy of the video *Places of the Heart* and cue it to the appropriate location. You may also need to gather resources from your denomination on its traditions and beliefs about the Lord's Supper. Be sure to read through the material and make your choices about options early enough so you have time to gather your supplies.

Note
1. Nick Page, *The Tabloid Bible* (Louisville: John Knox, 1998), pp.123, 136, 139.

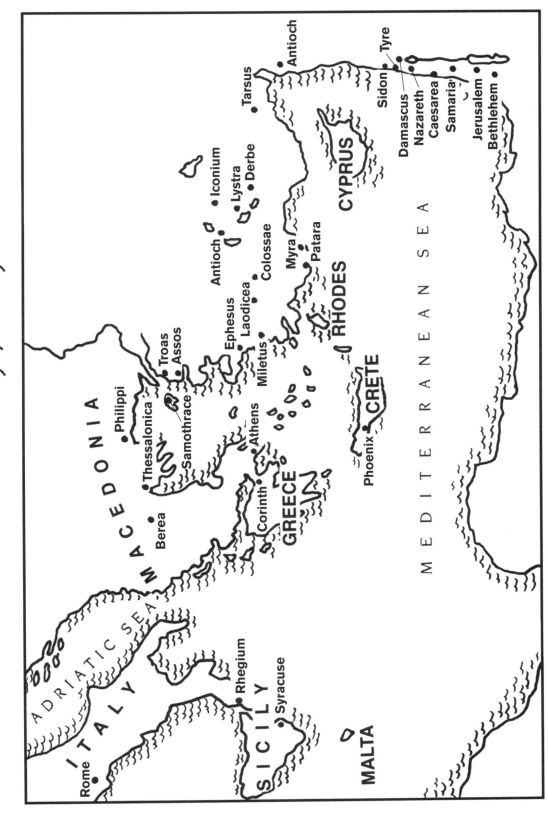

Paul's Missionary Journeys

Snapshots of Women in the Young Church

Acts 9:36-38
The ministry of Tabitha
(also called Dorcas), who
is named a disciple of Christ

Acts 12:12
The young church gathering in the
home of Mary the mother of John
(one of many patronesses of the church)

Acts 17:11-12
The conversion of prominent Greek
(or Gentile) women

Acts 18:1-2,18
Paul's partnership with Priscilla
and Aquila

Romans 16:1-6,13,15
Paul's greetings to several women who
helped him in his ministry

Philippians 4:3
Paul's commendation of the work
of two women

18. The Great Banquet

Bible Story: Luke 14:15-24

Rene Rodgers Jensen

A Story behind the Story

Throughout Jesus' ministry he made it clear that he was especially concerned about those on whom the society of his day (and ours!) looked down: the poor, the disabled, and the powerless, including women and children. While this is a theme in all four of the Gospels, it is especially prominent in the Gospel of Luke. It is in Luke's Gospel, for instance, that we have the story of Jesus' birth as a homeless child in a stable, surrounded not by the wealthy wise men of Matthew but by poor shepherds. Luke's Gospel also gives a particularly prominent role to women, who were virtually powerless in the society of Jesus' day.

The parable for this week's lesson reflects several characteristic themes of Jesus' ministry. First, it shows Jesus' particular concern for the poor and the outcast. Second, it suggests another theme we often see in the Gospels—the theme of reversal. Instead of the rich and powerful attending the banquet, the guests are the poor, the lame, and the blind. It is a vivid example of what Jesus meant when he said that "the last shall be first and the first last." Third, it offers the metaphor of salvation as being like a great party or banquet.

The occasion that elicits the parable is a party at the home of a religious leader. The parable for our study is actually the last in a series of teachings on that occasion. Jesus used the setting of a real banquet for a series of teachings that center on the metaphor of a banquet.

Jesus often taught in parables, or teaching stories. One common definition is that a parable is "an earthly story with a heavenly meaning." Jesus used everyday elements of life in his time—a shepherd and his sheep, a farmer putting in a crop, a dishonest employee—to make a point about the nature of God, the life of faith, God's justice, and the meaning of salvation. Parables are deceptively simple stories. They often seem quite straightforward. But many parables are really quite complex, with many layers of meaning. Different people at different times in their lives will hear a parable differently. This parable, like many of Jesus' parables, ends with a jolt—it is the most unexpected guests who end up at the banquet.

Enter the Story

Read all of Luke 14. Note how the Scripture for this lesson picks up themes suggested earlier in the chapter—the themes of a banquet and the role of the poor. It also sets the stage for the teachings on discipleship to follow. The lame excuses offered by the first party guests set the stage for what Jesus says in 14:25-35 about the conditions for following him.

As you reflect on your own life of faith, what are the excuses that you have given to God for not accepting God's invitation to the banquet? Is there something you are struggling with right now? Pray

- How open am I to people who are different than I am?
- What am I most likely to put ahead of God in my life?
- How often do I offer an excuse for not doing what I know is right?

YOU MAY NEED

- chalkboard or newsprint
- chalk or markers
- snacks
- nice dishes and napkins
- candles
- CD player
- CD of soft music
- formal clothing or apron (optional)
- Bibles
- "Guided Reflection" handout
- "An Important Invitation" handouts
- writing utensils
- TV and VCR
- *Places in the Heart* video, cued to the final scene of the Lord's Supper
- paper
- basket or offering tray

honestly for God's help in working through that issue.

Reflect on the youth in your class. Where are they in their relationship with God? What are the excuses—the barriers—that may be preventing them from taking the next step in that relationship? Keep these needs in mind as you continue preparation for this week's session.

Setting the Stage (5–10 minutes)

OPTION A

Needed: chalkboard and chalk or newsprint and markers

Ask the youth to come up with a top-ten list of lame excuses for not doing homework. To do this, first have the kids brainstorm excuses. List all excuses on the chalkboard or newsprint. Then have them vote on which ten excuses are the most outrageous. Rank them in order in true David Letterman fashion, from number ten to number one (encouraging *Late Night*–style applause, hoots, and whistles during the final reading).

Discuss with the youth how easy it is to come up with excuses for not doing something you do not want to do, such as homework or chores around the house. Explain that today you will be hearing a story Jesus told of when people came up with a lot of lame excuses.

OPTION B

Needed: snacks, nice dishes, napkins, candles, etc.; CD player; CD of soft music (optional); formal clothing or apron (optional)

Serve a snack in an elaborately formal manner. The snacks can just be doughnuts or some other simple food, but prepare the room as for a fancy party. Use nice dishes or pretty paper plates. Provide cloth napkins or higher-quality paper napkins. Arrange the snacks on a serving table in a more formal way. Use candles on the serving table and perhaps around the room. Play a CD of background music like the kind of music you would hear in a fine restaurant, such as violin music. You may even want to dress as a waiter by wearing a white apron or a black tie. Pretend to be the maitre d' of a fine restaurant, ushering the youth into the room in an over-the-top, black-tie-only way.

Invite the youth to respond to how it feels to have their snacks served in such a special way. Do they like it, or does it make them feel uncomfortable?

Ask the youth if they have ever been to a really fancy restaurant. What was it like? Have the youth remember the best meal they ever had. What made it so memorable?

Explain that today you will be talking about a story that Jesus told of a very special banquet.

Telling the Story (5–10 minutes)

Before either option, explain to the class that today's Scripture is a parable. Jesus told many parables. A parable is a teaching story. Give the youth the definition offered in "A Story behind the Story": "an earthly story with a heavenly meaning." This means that Jesus used common, everyday things of his day, like giving a party, to explain something about God and what God wants of us.

OPTION A
Needed: Bibles
Divide the youth into three groups (a group can be just one person). Assign each group the responsibility of hearing the story from the perspective of one of the players in the drama. Ask one group to listen to the story and imagine how the banquet host felt. Ask the second group to hear the story from the perspective of one of those initially invited to the banquet. Try to understand what is going on with this person. The third group will think about what it would have been like to have been a poor, crippled beggar who received such an unexpected invitation.

Read the story. Then ask the different groups to respond to the following questions:
Host
- How do you feel as you begin to plan for your banquet?
- How do you feel when your guests all turn you down?
- Will you invite them to a party in the future?
Guest who received first invitation
- How do you feel when you get the invitation to the banquet?
- Why do you turn it down?
- Do you care how this will make the host feel?
Poor Guest
- How do you feel when you get the invitation to come to a big banquet?
- When was the last time you had a decent meal?
- Why do you think the host invited you and the other poor,

crippled, and blind people to the feast?

OPTION B
Needed: "Guided Reflection" handout, Bibles
Read the Scripture while the youth follow along in their own Bibles and then read the guided reflection. The guided reflection tells the story from the point of view of the two different groups of guests. Read the reflection slowly and with feeling. Afterward, ask the youth to describe the feelings they imagined for the different persons in the story. With whom did they most identify? Why?

Reacting to the Story (10–15 minutes)
OPTION A
Needed: "An Important Invitation" handouts, writing utensils
Ask the youth to decide who the players in this parable represent. Who is the host supposed to be? Who is the first set of guests? Who is the second set of guests?

Discuss with the youth this question: *What do you think the point of this parable is supposed to be?*

Ask the youth to reflect on the emotions they identified with the characters in "Telling the Story." As they think about the symbolic significance of the different persons in the parable, does that change the emotions they identified with each of those groups? Why or why not?

Give each youth a copy of the handout, "An Important Invitation," and a writing utensil. Have them fill in the invitation with their response to the question "What is God inviting us to?" (They should write it as if writing an actual invitation.)

Afterward, discuss the following questions with the youth:
- What did you put on the invitation that God invites us to? Why?
- To whom does God send this invitation?

OPTION B

Needed: TV and VCR, video of Places in the Heart *(cued as described below)*

Explain the story of *Places in the Heart:* Sally Field plays a widow in Texas during the Depression. Her sheriff husband was killed by a young black man, who shot him accidentally. The men of the small Texas town where she lives lynched the young black man.

In order to keep her farm and earn a living for her two young children, the widow harvests a cotton crop. She enlists the help of a blind boarder and a black hired hand (played by Danny Glover). They succeed in bringing in their cotton crop before anyone else, winning a bonus from the cotton mill. This brings out resentment from the established farmers. They run off the hired hand.

Play the final scene from the movie, which is the sharing of the Lord's Supper in the church. Here the view gradually reveals that what we are seeing is not an actual church service but a glimpse of God's intention for the world. In this rigidly segregated society, you see blacks and whites worshiping together. You even see the murdered sheriff passing Communion to the young man who killed him. Ask the youth to discuss how this

scene is like the banquet from Luke 14.

Connecting to the Story (10–15 minutes)

OPTION A

Needed: newsprint, markers

Ask the youth to describe how heaven is usually portrayed. They will probably mention things like angels with wings, pearly gates, streets of gold, and so forth. Explain that Jesus often talked about heaven as a great banquet or a wedding feast. In other words, heaven is like a big party.

Using the idea of a party, have the youth come up with a description of heaven. Use the following points to help them come up with their description. Keep track of their ideas on newsprint.

Good party planners say that every party needs a theme. What would be the theme of the party?
- What would the decorations be like?
- We usually think about wearing white robes, halos, and wings in heaven. If heaven is a party, what do you wear?
- What do you eat at this party?
- Who is invited to the party?
- If heaven is a party, how would it be different than even the greatest earthly party?
- Why would anyone turn down an invitation to this party?

If you have time and the opportunity, consider having the youth use their plans to throw an actual party for the children's classes, senior citizens, a women's or men's group, the pastor, or someone else in the church. But remind them to follow their theme if they do so!

152

OPTION B
Needed: newsprint, markers

Using some of the information from "A Story behind the Story," explain that Jesus made it clear throughout his ministry that he has a special care for the poor, the outcast, and the marginalized in our society. Ask the youth to explain how this concern is reflected in this parable.

Invite the youth to rewrite the parable using a contemporary situation. Below are questions you can use in helping them translate the parable to today.

■ Who would be the host of the banquet?
■ What would the host be inviting people to attend?
■ Who would be the first set of guests?
■ What kinds of excuses would they offer?
■ Who would be the second set of guests?
■ Where would the last guests come from?

Write down on newsprint all the images the kids have come up with and retell the story, substituting what they said.

_____ gave a great _____.
_____ invited _____.

But when _____ received the invitation, they said they couldn't come because _____ or _____ or _____.

So _____ invited _____ instead. But there was still room for more people, so _____ asked _____ to come to the _____.

Exploring the Story
(10–15 minutes)
OPTION A
Needed: Bibles

Using some of the background material from "A Story behind the Story," explain that the care of the poor, the outcast, and the marginalized in society was always a special theme in Jesus' ministry.

Have the youth look up the following passages from Luke's Gospel and discuss the following questions:

■ **Luke 4:16-21:** This passage describes Jesus' first sermon. It is his first public statement about his ministry and what his ministry will be about. What does he say that God is asking him to do?
■ **Luke 6:20-26:** This is Luke's version of the more familiar Sermon on the Mount, which is found in the Gospel of Matthew. Who does Jesus say is blessed? Who does Jesus say is cursed?
■ **Luke 9:46-58:** What does Jesus say it means to be great?
■ **Luke 14:12-14:** Who does Jesus say should be invited to the banquet?

After you have read and discussed the various Scriptures, ask the youth what these Scriptures, along with the parable, say about Jesus. Then ask: *What do these Scriptures tell us about how we should live our lives? What do all these Scriptures suggest about what God wants from the church?*

OPTION B
Needed: denominational resource about the Lord's Supper

For this option, you may need to ask your pastor or look in the church library for a resource that

153

explains your denomination's beliefs about the Lord's Supper.

Explain to the youth that Jesus often used the image of a banquet or wedding feast in his teaching. He often gathered with people around a meal. (Jesus was at a party at the home of a prominent religious leader when he told this parable.) In fact, Jesus went to so many parties that his enemies accused him of being a drunkard and a glutton (Luke 7:34).

In that tradition, most churches enjoy getting together around food. Have the youth brainstorm all the events in your church during the course of a year that involve eating. (Examples could range from weekly coffee hour to potluck dinners to special church programs). Ask, *Why do you think so many events in the life of our church revolve around eating?*

Say that one of the central practices of the Christian faith is participation in the Lord's Supper. Explain some central aspects about what your denomination teaches about the Lord's Supper. Ask:

■ Why do you suppose Jesus chose a meal as the main way for us to remember him?

■ How do you see the main points of the parable reflected in what we believe about the Lord's Supper?

Living the Story (5–10 minutes)

OPTION A

Needed: pieces of paper, writing utensils, candle, matches or lighter, basket or tray

Place the candle on a small table and light it. Put a basket or tray in front of the candle. Have the group gather in a circle around the table. Say that today's parable is about people who offered excuses for not accepting an invitation to a great party. Ask the group to think of excuses that people use for not accepting God's invitation to the banquet of abundant life. Have them focus in particular on the kinds of excuses that persons of their age offer.

Then ask each of the youth to think of what excuse they have been giving for not taking the next step in their life of faith. What is the barrier to their going deeper in their relationship with Jesus Christ? Ask them to write that excuse on the piece of paper. Have the youth come forward and place their papers in the basket or tray as a way of saying that they want to move beyond excuses into a deeper relationship with Christ.

End with a prayer for God's help in overcoming excuses and responding with our whole hearts to God's invitation.

OPTION B

Needed: candle, matches or lighter

Place a lit candle on a table in the center of the room and have the group gather around it. Ask the youth to respond to each phrase by saying in unison, "Remind us we are your children."

■ When we get so busy that we don't have time for you . . .

■ When we look down on others . . .

■ When we begin to believe the worst . . .

■ When we are afraid . . .

■ When we feel weak . . .

■ When it is difficult to accept those who are different . . .

- When we think anything is more important than you . . .
- When we take for granted all the good things in our lives . . .
- When we have hurt others' feelings . . .
- When we put anything ahead of you . . .
- When we think caring for the poor is someone else's job . . .
- When being popular is more important than being kind . . .
- When we have taken your love for granted . . .

Things to Ponder

Soon after the session, reflect on what happened. Where did the youth respond particularly well? Studying the invitation and Lord's Supper can raise issues of inclusion and exclusion for the youth. Did any personal concerns or issues arise that need follow-up? If so, make a note to call or e-mail members of the group in the coming week to check in with them.

Looking Ahead

You will need to find a good video on early church history prior to the next session. The session itself lists some suggestions. Try your local church resource center first, or check at a public library or the library of a local seminary or university. If such sources are not available to you, there are several places online you can go to order such videos. You will also need to find appropriate music for one of the options, and you will need to collect current newspapers and news magazines during the week. Make sure you plan ahead for these things.

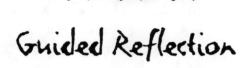

Guided Reflection

To be read aloud by the leader only.

You are a rich person. You are very busy. You have the money to go anywhere and do anything. You get an invitation from one of your friends. You say you will go, but then you get another invitation. It is from someone even richer and more important than you are. You are flattered and excited to receive this second invitation. Then you realize that the party will be on the same night as your friend's party. You start to think of some excuse that will get you out of your friend's party. It might hurt your friend's feelings, but you tell yourself that he'll get over it. When the day of the party comes, you send word that you can't make it.

You are a poor beggar. You hurt your leg five years ago and haven't been able to work since. You beg for money and food. You usually beg outside the home of a rich man, and you mainly live off scraps from the rich man's kitchen. You are hungry most of the time. It has been years since you had a full stomach and a decent meal. One evening, as you are about to make your bed under a tree near the rich man's house, a servant comes rushing out. He says the rich man wants you to come inside for a banquet. At first you think he is joking, but he insists. In wonder, you enter the rich man's home. Spread before you is the most glorious food you can imagine. All around you are people just like you—the poor, the crippled, the blind. You are greeted with honor and ushered to a place of honor. You are treated as if you were the most important person in town.

An Important Invitation

19. Hunger and Thirst No More

Bible Story: Revelation 7:9-17

Rene Rodgers Jensen

A Story behind the Story

Perhaps no book in the entire Bible has been so misunderstood and misinterpreted as the Book of Revelation. Its obscure symbolism has puzzled and enticed readers for centuries. Many others are put off by its bloody depictions of an apocalyptic struggle or intimidated by its strange symbolism.

Revelation is perhaps the preeminent example of apocalyptic writing. Apocalypticism deals with the end of time. It typically portrays a cosmic struggle between the forces of light and the forces of darkness. The new age of God's perfect reign will be ushered in through this struggle. We live in the midst of that struggle, but the outcome is never in doubt. God's ultimate victory is assured.

The key to understanding Revelation is understanding the context within which it was written. It was written toward the end of the first century to encourage a young church that was undergoing great persecution. The Roman Empire—the greatest empire the world has ever known—was intent on wiping out this troublesome sect. The Christians, who were mainly slaves, the poor, women, and other marginalized persons, seemed to have little chance to withstand the mighty Roman Empire.

John wrote the Book of Revelation to give courage to the Christian community. He used the images of a cosmic struggle between the forces of good and evil, light and dark, to help them understand that they were taking part in this struggle. Revelation shows that in this great struggle the forces of good, the forces of God, will ultimately triumph. By showing that the final victory is assured, Revelation is intended to help Christians stand firm despite the threat of persecution. Revelation 7 is one of several passages that depict the glories awaiting those who stay faithful by withstanding the forces of evil arrayed against them.

Revelation is often misused to interpret contemporary events, but John was writing to a first-century community. He used symbols and images that had meaning for that time and place. This certainly does not suggest that Revelation has no meaning for contemporary Christians. The underlying message of Revelation—that there is a great and ongoing battle between the forces of good and evil, and that we are to be a part of God's army in that struggle—is as relevant for us as it was for John's original audience.

Enter the Story

People are often intimidated by the thought of teaching from the Book of Revelation, believing that one has to be an expert Bible scholar to interpret its strange and sometimes bizarre imagery. But the basic message of Revelation is simple: God is in charge. Good will triumph.

This session is being written during a tense time in our country and in our world, while the events of September 11 and our war with Afghanistan are fresh in our experience. Some time will have passed by the time you are leading this session, but the experience will linger. The Book of Revelation is a good place to go at a time of anxiety. It was written to comfort a community that was under attack and for whom the future was uncertain. The powerful message of Revelation is that no matter how strong evil may look, God will eventually triumph.

Setting the Stage
(5–10 minutes)
OPTION A
Needed: magazine pictures of people dressed in different ways
Before class, collect pictures of people dressed in ways that might suggest something about their occupation (for example, a doctor or nurse, a police officer), their economic status (someone richly dressed, a person dressed in rags), their hobby (sports clothing), and so on. Show the pictures to the class. Ask them to say what they can tell about the people by the way they are dressed. What are the clues we get to someone's lifestyle or personality by the way they dress?

Invite the youth to talk about how the kids dress at their schools. Ask: *How do the different cliques dress? Why? What is your own favorite outfit? What do you feel most comfortable in? Why? What do our clothes reveal about us?*

Some churches expect members to dress in a certain way. Does your church have an unwritten dress code? What is it? Why? If not, why not?

Mention that some religious groups dress in a distinctive way. For example, the Amish and some branches of the Mennonite and

Brethren have a distinctive way of dressing. Priests and some ministers dress in a clerical collar. Some Jewish men wear a yarmulke. Some Muslim women wear head coverings

Ask: *What would be the advantages of having Christians dress in an identifying way? What would be the disadvantages?*

OPTION B
Needed: "Signs of the Times" handouts, paper, writing utensils
Copy the handout and cut apart the different symbols. Give one or more symbols to each member of the group. Ask them to tell what each symbol stands for. Can they name some more symbols they see everyday? Ask them to name some specifically Christian symbols.

Give everyone a piece of paper and a writing utensil. Give them two minutes to write a sentence using only symbols. Have them share their symbol sentences with one another.

Did they have trouble understanding what the symbol sentences meant? Can symbols be a kind of secret code?

Explain to the class that today's Scripture story is full of symbols. Sometimes these symbols can make something difficult to understand, but at other times, symbols can provide a depth of meaning that mere words cannot express.

Telling the Story
(5–10 minutes)
Before reading the Scripture in either option below, share some of the information from "A Story behind the Story" about the Book of Revelation. Explain that the Roman Empire persecuted the early

POSSIBLE YOUTH CONTACT POINTS
- Where am I tempted to forsake my faith?
- Where do I feel a part of the struggle for good?
- Where do I feel God's blessing in my life?

YOU MAY NEED
- magazine pictures of people dressed in different ways
- "Signs of the Times" handouts
- paper
- writing utensils
- Bibles
- CD player
- CD of triumphant music
- newsprint or chalkboard
- markers or chalk
- newspapers and news magazines
- "Just Desserts" handouts
- video about the history of the early church
- TV and VCR
- candles
- matches or lighter
- basket or offering tray

Christians for the first three hundred years of its existence.

The Romans required everyone who lived under the empire's power (which was most of the known world) to worship the emperor as a god. For most people in the Roman Empire, who worshiped many gods, worshiping Caesar was not much of a problem. The Jewish people had a special dispensation from Rome, due to careful working with the empire to keep Caesar happy. Christians, however, worshiped only one God—the God revealed to the world through Jesus Christ. They refused to worship the emperor as a god. Christians said they would gladly pray *for* the emperor but would not pray *to* the emperor.

Since the Christians were a new sect to the empire, they had no long-standing tradition. In addition, the religion itself set comfortable boundaries between master and slave on its ears. Because of this refusal and its dangerous teachings, the Roman Empire was intent on wiping out the Christian faith.

Explain that visions of heaven such as we see in Revelation 7 were meant to give hope and strength to Christians who lived in fear of persecution.

OPTION A
Needed: Bibles, CD of triumphant music, CD player
Divide the group up to read the Scripture as a choral reading. Assign the following parts: narrator, the multitude, the angels, the elder. Have the music playing in the background while the group reads the Scripture. Encourage

them to use expression in creating a sense of triumph and exultation.

After you have completed the reading, discuss the following questions.
■ Who made up the multitude? What does it mean that they were from every nation and people?
■ What do you think is the significance of the white robes? Of the palm branches?
■ Who is the Lamb?
■ What qualifies those in the white robes to stand before God?

OPTION B
Needed: Bibles, newsprint, markers
Read through the Scripture passage. Hand out the markers and have the group draw a mural of the scene described in the passage on the newsprint. Help them plan the mural by asking the following questions:
■ What should be in the center?
■ Where are the angels? The elders? The multitude?
■ What is the multitude doing? Wearing? Holding?

Remind them that artistic ability is not the point here. They should simply try to get a representation of the Scripture story down in pictorial form.

Reacting to the Story (10–15 minutes)
OPTION A
(This is a good follow-up to Option B of "Setting the Stage.")
Needed: Bible, newsprint or chalkboard, markers or chalk, multicolored construction paper, writing utensils, scissors
Explain to the group that much of Revelation is told through the use

of symbols. Ask someone to read through the passage once again, pausing after each verse. Have the group name symbols that are in each verse (some verses may not have symbols). Write the symbols on the chalkboard or newsprint. Ask the group what they think each of the symbols means.

Ask each youth to decide on a color that they think fits the mood of the Scripture passage. Choose that color from the construction paper provided. Then ask them to decide on a symbol that seems to fit the mood of the passage. This does not have to be a symbol specifically mentioned in the passage, but rather it can be a symbolic representation of how the writer of Revelation wants his hearers to feel after they have heard this story read. Ask them to draw that symbol on the construction paper and cut it out. Remind them that they do not have to be great artists—they just need to get an approximate semblance of the symbol.

Have the group pair off. Ask each person to explain to his or her partner why that person chose this symbol to represent the mood of the passage.

OPTION B
Needed: Bibles, paper, writing utensils
Remind the group that the passage refers to "the great tribulation" (see verse 14) through which the multitude has come. Bible scholars usually interpret this to refer to the persecution that Christians experienced at the hands of the Roman Empire. Discuss the following questions:

■ If you were a Christian undergoing persecution in the first or second century, would this picture of heaven give you encouragement? Why or why not?
■ What are the images of victory and triumph that the passage offers?
■ Look again at verses 15-17. What is promised to the faithful multitude?

In our country, Christians do not live under the threat of persecution. We are blessed to live in a nation where we can freely practice our religion. However, this does not mean we are not tempted to turn our back on God. Divide into groups of two or three. Have each group come up with a list of things that may tempt us away from God.

Connecting to the Story (10–15 minutes)
OPTION A
Needed: newspapers and news magazines from previous week
Explain that Revelation is an example of what is called "apocalyptic writing." Apocalyptic writing talks about the end times. It often uses the imagery of a great battle between the forces of God and Satan, good and evil, light and dark. When Revelation was written, the writer saw that battle being waged between the persecuted Christians and the Roman Empire.

The battle between good and evil goes on today. Christians are still being asked to struggle against the forces of darkness in the world. Hand out the newspapers and news magazines. Ask the youth to look for stories of the struggle between good and evil.

It is well to extend a small caution in this exercise. We are all tempted to believe that God is on our side—politically, socially, economically. It is far too easy to decide that someone who disagrees with us or is different from us is evil. Encourage the youth to avoid the temptation to use God to baptize their own political or social opinions. Rather, they should genuinely struggle with discerning God's will for our world.

Ask the youth to look in the newspaper for ways in which they can see God's struggle unfolding in our world. How can people of faith be a part of that struggle?

OPTION B

Needed: "Just Desserts" handouts, writing utensils

Revelation 7 is about the reward that the faithful will receive in the life to come. This option gives the youth the opportunity to discuss how they understand God's judgment. Does God judge us? Is that judgment exclusively after death, or do we receive judgment in this lifetime as well? Christians hold many different beliefs about these types of issues.

Make copies of the handout for each person in the group. Ask them to put a check mark beside each statement with which they agree. Have them put an X beside each statement with which they disagree. Ask them to put a question mark beside the statements they are not sure about.

Give them a few minutes to complete the exercise. Stress that there are not really right or wrong answers. After they are finished, discuss their responses. Encourage

them to explain their answers, if they are comfortable sharing.

Exploring the Story (10–15 minutes)

OPTION A

Needed: Bibles

Revelation 7 is a picture of God's final victory, of how the world will look when God's will is truly done on earth as it is in heaven. The Bible presents several depictions of what this perfected existence will look like. Depending on the size of your group, assign one or two youth to look up each of the following Scriptures:

■ **Isaiah 25:6-10:** Isaiah's vision is of God giving a great banquet to which all the world is invited.

■ **Isaiah 65:17-25:** Here is a picture of perfect peace and harmony, in which even ancient enemies, such as the wolf and the lamb, eat together in peace.

■ **Jeremiah 31:31-34:** Jeremiah speaks of a time when the knowledge of God is so perfect that there is no need to teach about God.

■ **Matthew 24:15-31:** This is a foreboding vision of the final battle and Christ's triumphant return.

■ **John 3:16-21:** Among the most beloved and familiar of all New Testament passages, these verses explain what is needed to attain eternal life.

■ **1 Corinthians 15:50-56:** Paul wrestles with the mystery of death and resurrection.

■ **Revelation 21:1-8:** John presents another vision of the end times.

Invite the youth to read their assigned Scripture or Scriptures and be prepared to answer the following questions:

- How is the vision presented in these Scriptures similar to Revelation 7?
- How is it different?

OPTION B
Needed: video about early church history, TV and VCR
Check your church library or public library for videos related to the early history of the church. The Arts and Entertainment Network has an excellent series called *Christianity: The First Thousand Years* (A&E Home Video, 1998), which is available in some libraries or from Web sites such as Barnes & Noble (www.bn.com). Show a clip from the video that deals with the persecution of Christians under the Roman Empire.

Discuss the following questions:
- Where did early Christians find the courage to stay true to their faith in the face of persecution?
- Do you think early Christians truly believed that they were stronger than the Roman Empire?
- Oddly enough, the courage with which Christians accepted their punishment was a powerful witness. Many of those who witnessed the public executions of the Christians were so impressed by what they saw that they became Christians themselves. Why do you think this was true?
- Do you think Christians today in our country would have the courage to stand up to persecution? Why or why not?
- Here's an old question: If you were arrested for being a Christian, would there be enough evidence to convict you? What is the "evidence" we look for that someone is a Christian?

Living the Story
(5–10 minutes)
OPTION A
Needed: candles, matches or lighter, basket or offering tray, pieces of paper, writing utensils
Place the lit candle on a small table. Put the basket or offering tray by the candle. Gather the group around the candle. Thank them for their participation in the day's learning.

Remind them that the temptation to turn your back on Christ is just as real today as it was nearly two thousand years ago when the Book of Revelation was being written. Reiterate the point that there is an ongoing battle between good and evil in our world today (defined however you and your tradition define it) and that we continue to be a part of that great struggle. You may want to make specific references to some of your discussion earlier on these points.

Give each youth a piece of paper and a writing utensil. Ask them to write on the paper how they feel they are tempted to be unfaithful to their commitment to Christ. Do not ask them to share what they wrote but rather to quietly place their paper in the basket or tray.

Close with prayer asking for God's strength to stand firm in the faith in the days to come.

OPTION B
(If this is the last session you are using for the year's theme of Justice and Liberation, this would be a good final closure.)
Needed: chalkboard and chalk or newsprint and markers
Remind the group that today's Scripture story once again lifts up

God's ultimate concern for the poor and oppressed. Read verses 16 and 17 again. What is our role in justice and liberation? How are we called, in our faith, to reflect God's concern for the poor and oppressed? Ask the group to brainstorm ways to show their faith in the coming week, months, or year. Write their suggestions on the chalkboard or newsprint. After a few minutes, ask each youth to indicate which of these ways he or she would be willing to commit to in the coming week.

Stand in a prayer circle. Ask each person to pray for the person on his or her left, that God will give that one the strength, faith, and courage in the coming week to be faithful to the commitment to act on faith.

Things to Ponder

Soon after the session, reflect on the past year's sessions with the youth. Where did the youth respond particularly well? What didn't seem to work at all? Reflect on your own leadership. What did you do well? What could you improve? Be sure to make plans for the next quarter early!

Signs of the Times

Just Desserts

Put a check mark by every statement you agree with.
Put an X by every statement that you disagree with.
Put a question mark by statements that you are not sure about.

_____ **Our actions don't really matter much one way or the other. There is no such thing as judgment.**

_____ **God watches every move we make and writes down any of our sins. If we sin a certain amount, we are doomed to hell for eternity.**

_____ **God rewards and punishes us only in this life.**

_____ **God rewards and punishes us only after our death.**

_____ **God rewards and punishes us both in this life and in the life to come.**

_____ **Even after death, God continues to offer the invitation to our souls to be unified with God. Someone who is not saved in this life might still have the chance to be saved after death.**

_____ **We get into heaven because we live a good life.**

_____ **We get into heaven because of Jesus Christ.**

_____ **Only Christians will go to heaven.**

_____ **We are saved by grace.**

_____ **We are saved by our good works.**

_____ **If we truly believe in God, then we will show that belief by the way we live our lives.**

BibleQuest Bookmark Stories Index

Year 1	Bookmark Story	Title	Corresponding Lesson
Fall	Genesis 1:1–2:4a	Creation	Vol. 3, Lesson 1
	Exodus 3:1-12	The Burning Bush	Vol. 1, Lesson 10
	1 Samuel 16:1-13	David Chosen King	Vol. 6, Lesson 1
	Isaiah 11:1-9	Peaceable Kingdom	Vol. 1, Lesson 13
Winter	Matthew 1:18-24	Joseph's Dream	Vol. 1, Lesson 16
	Mark 1:1-11	Jesus' Baptism	Vol. 6, Lesson 2
Spring	John 20:1-18	Women at the Tomb	Vol. 6, Lesson 3
	Revelation 21:1-7	God Always with Us	Vol. 6, Lesson 4
Summer	Psalm 150	A Psalm of Praise	Vol. 6, Lesson 5
	Psalm 23	Shepherd Psalm	Vol. 4, Lesson 2
	Luke 10:38–11:4	Prayer Jesus Taught	Vol. 6, Lesson 6

Year 2	Bookmark Story	Title	Corresponding Lesson
Fall	Genesis 2:4b-25	Creation	Vol. 6, Lesson 7
	Genesis 7–8	Noah	Vol. 6, Lesson 8
	Genesis 17:1-27	Abraham and Sarah	Vol. 1, Lesson 2
	Exodus 20:1-21	Ten Commandments	Vol. 6, Lesson 9
Winter	Ruth 1–4	Ruth	Vol. 2, Lesson 3
	2 Samuel 7:1-17	Covenant with David	Vol. 4, Lesson 1
	2 Kings 22	Josiah and Huldah	Vol. 6, Lesson 10
	Jeremiah 31:31-34	Jeremiah	Vol. 6, Lesson 11
Spring	Mark 2:23-28	Jesus and the Sabbath	Vol. 6, Lesson 12
	Luke 24:13-35	Emmaus Road	Vol. 6, Lesson 13
	Acts 2	Pentecost	Vol. 4, Lesson 13
	Hebrews 11:1–12:2	Cloud of Witnesses	Vol. 6, Lesson 14
Summer	Psalm 105	God's Faithfulness	Vol. 6, Lesson 15
	Psalm 8	Psalm of Creation	Vol. 6, Lesson 16
	John 6:1-14	Feeding the 5,000	Vol. 6, Lesson 17

Year 3	Bookmark Story	Title	Corresponding Lesson
Fall	Genesis 18:1-15	Welcome Strangers	Vol. 5, Lesson 1
	Exodus 2:1-12; 12–14	Exodus	Vol. 1, Lesson 9
	2 Kings 4:1-37	Elisha and the Widow's Oil	Vol. 5, Lesson 2
	Micah 4:1-8	Reign of God	Vol. 5, Lesson 3

Year 3 (cont.)	Bookmark Story	Title	Corresponding Lesson
Winter	Luke 1:39-56	Mary's Song	Vol. 3, Lesson 13
	Luke 4:16-30	Jesus' Announcement	Vol. 2, Lesson 5
	Luke 10:25-37	The Good Samaritan	Vol. 2, Lesson 4
	Luke 16:19-31	Rich Man and Lazarus	Vol. 3, Lesson 7
Spring	Matthew 20:20-28	Seeking Honor	Vol. 5, Lesson 4
	Matthew 22:34-40	Great Commandment	Vol. 5, Lesson 5
	Matthew 25:31-46	The Least of These	Vol. 2, Lesson 8
	Philemon	Onesimus	Vol. 5, Lesson 6
Summer	Jeremiah 18:1-6	The Potter's Wheel	Vol. 5, Lesson 7
	Matthew 4:23–5:16	Sermon on the Mount	Vol. 5, Lesson 8
	James 1:22–2:26	Doers, Not Just Hearers	Vol. 5, Lesson 9

Year 4	Bookmark Story	Title	Corresponding Lesson
Fall	Genesis 3	Problems in the Garden	Vol. 1, Lesson 1
	Genesis 39:1-3; 45:1–46:7	Joseph	Vol. 5, Lesson 10
	Joshua 3–4	Joshua	Vol. 5, Lesson 11
	1 Samuel 25	Abigail	Vol. 5, Lesson 12
Winter	Jonah 1–4	Jonah	Vol. 5, Lesson 13
	Luke 2:25-38	Simeon and Anna	Vol. 5, Lesson 14
	John 3:1-21	Nicodemus	Vol. 1, Lesson 5
	Luke 19:1-10	Zacchaeus	Vol. 1, Lesson 8
Spring	Mark 14:3-9	Anointing at Bethany	Vol. 5, Lesson 15
	John 20:19-29	Thomas Hears Good News	Vol. 5, Lesson 16
	Acts 9:1-19a	Saul's Conversion	Vol. 4, Lesson 15
	Acts 16:11-40	Lydia; Paul and Silas in Prison	Vol. 5, Lesson 17
Summer	Daniel 6:6-23	Daniel in Lion's Den	Vol. 4, Lesson 3
	Luke 14:15-24	Great Banquet	Vol. 5, Lesson 18
	Revelation 7:9-17	Every Nation	Vol. 5, Lesson 19